Praise for

His Other Life

Part *noir* thriller, part forensic memoir, one hundred percent page-turning literary journalism, *His Other Life* leads you down numerous dark and narrow corridors, real and imagined, to reconstruct the life and death of Hazel Kramer—and of all who knew and loved her. You enter looking for Tennessee Williams, but you leave having found Melanie McCabe.

—John S. Bak, Université de Lorraine,

author of *Tennessee Williams: A Literary Life*

His Other Life is a compelling read. Melanie McCabe has combined rigorous research and her own personal journey into an excellent tale. *His Other Life* adds significant information to the biography of Tennessee Williams during his formative period in St. Louis. Literary fans will enjoy the fascinating details about Hazel Kramer, Terrence McCabe and Tennessee Williams. They were energetic young college students in the 1930s, but circumstances pulled their lives in disparate directions. Their story is a reflection of a particular time and place in our history that is not so well known. Seldom have I read a book that so vividly portrays the pursuit of historical details and archival research. The facts of her father's life are not abstractions, but are complex emotional discoveries.

—Prof. Tom Mitchell,

Tennessee Williams Scholar, University of Illinois

As is often the case in trying to retrace the past, certain questions simply remain unanswered. Letters are lost or destroyed, recollections fade, and key clues lie moldering in a trunk in someone's attic. Nonetheless, McCabe's eloquent determination to investigate this mystery—sleuthing online, contacting descendants, and entering archives full of "carbon paper and ghosts"—gives *His Other Life* a historical and literary resonance that is charged with modern energy.

—Meg Nola, Foreword Reviews

University of New Orleans Press
Manufactured in the United States of America
All rights reserved

ISBN: 9786-0801134-65

All images courtesy of Melanie McCabe unless otherwise noted.
Book and cover design by Alex Dimeff.

Portions of this book were previously published in *Shenandoah: The Washington and Lee University Review*.

This is a work of nonfiction. The author has drawn from a number of sources, including media articles and investigations, legal transcripts, and interviews. It is also a memoir, which is to say that the story, the experiences, and the words are the author's alone. Dialogue has been re-created from memory. Names of certain characters have been changed to protect their privacy.

Library of Congress Cataloging-in-Publication Data

Names: McCabe, Melanie, 1957-
Title: His other life : searching for my father, his first wife, and
    Tennessee Williams / by Melanie McCabe.
Description: New Orleans : University of New Orleans Press, 2017.
Identifiers: LCCN 2017004006 | ISBN 9781608011346 (pbk.)
Subjects: LCSH: McCabe, Melanie, 1957---Family. | Williams, Tennessee,
    1911-1983.
Classification: LCC PS3613.C3236 Z46 2017 | DDC 811/.6 [B] --dc23

THE UNIVERSITY OF NEW ORLEANS PRESS
unopress.org

His Other Life

SEARCHING FOR MY FATHER, HIS FIRST WIFE,
AND TENNESSEE WILLIAMS

MELANIE McCABE

UNO PRESS

ACKNOWLEDGMENTS

I am deeply grateful to the following people for their assistance, support, and advice given to me during the course of my research and the writing of this book:

Annie Noble, Chris Perkowski, John Bak, Robert Bray, Francesca Williams, Jennifer Atkinson, Eric Pankey, David Ebenbach, David Taylor, Angie Chuang, Emily Mitchell, Bruce Henderson, Jackie Vaughan, Cindy Bagby, Nancy Bagby, Debbie Bagby, Sumner Bagby, Esme Gibson, Lory White Campagna, Raymond White, Anne Hughes, Thomas Hughes, Eleanor Keane, Sue Keane, Francine Barclay, Mia Mather, Linnell Mather, Roberta McCabe Morningstar, Ginger Marlatt, Natalie Shutler, Kathy Dull, Mark Templeton, Michael Frost, Joan Romadka Wilkie, Kimberley Sulik, Arlene Balkansky, Allan Mustard, David Langbart, Danielle Deulen, the staff at the National Archive, Chicago Branch, and the staff and administrators of the Virginia Center for the Creative Arts.

Profound gratitude to the University of New Orleans Press for choosing my book, and for those who had such a significant and valuable role in bringing it to publication: Abram Himelstein, George K. Darby, Katie Pfalzgraff, Tori Bush, Thomas Dollbaum, Ashley Hamrick, LB Kovac, Jeanne McGlory, Heidi McKinley, Jacob Reecher, Christine Stevralia, Glennis Waterman, and Megan Wetta.

And last, but most assuredly not least, to Christopher Winters, whose casual question ignited the research for this book, and whose unswerving support helped to keep me going.

In loving memory of my father, Terrence McCabe, who lived this story, and of my sister, Terri McCabe Nagel, who had hoped to live long enough to see me uncover it.

CONTENTS

The Story Waiting to be Told................................13

A Character Named Terrence McCabe..........................29

Three Childhoods..51

The Distant Hill..71

Hazel Asks For Help...91

Down In Mexico...103

Families, Destroyed and Repaired...........................159

Hazel's Day in Court.......................................171

The Mystery Man..181

Pretend It Never Happened..................................195

Something Cloudy Becomes Clear.............................203

The Mystery Women..217

Mr. McCabe Goes To Washington..............................231

Letting Go...239

Images...131

Bibliography...255

Endnotes...263

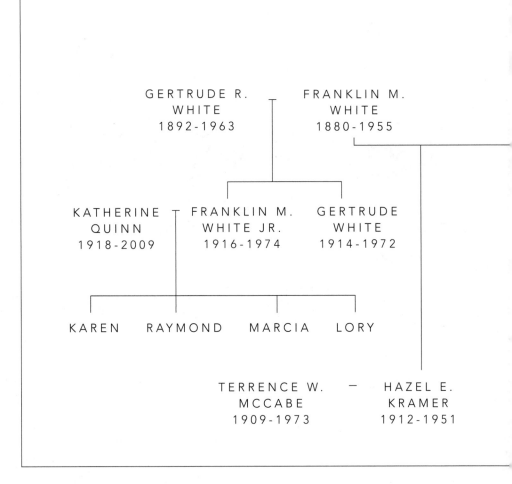

GERTRUDE R.
WHITE
1892-1963

FRANKLIN M.
WHITE
1880-1955

KATHERINE
QUINN
1918-2009

FRANKLIN M.
WHITE JR.
1916-1974

GERTRUDE
WHITE
1914-1972

KAREN   RAYMOND   MARCIA   LORY

TERRENCE W.   —   HAZEL E.
MCCABE   KRAMER
1909-1973   1912-1951

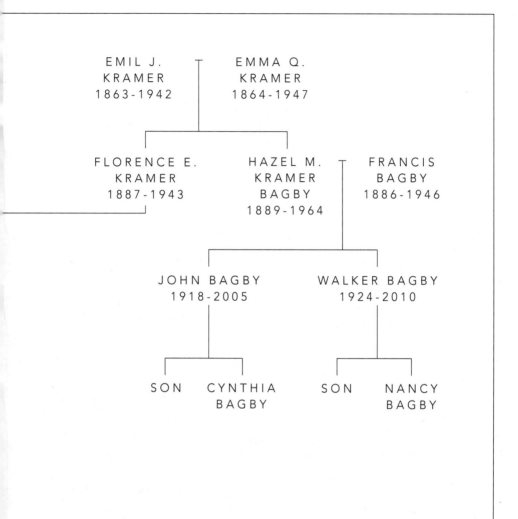

EMIL J.
KRAMER
1863-1942

EMMA Q.
KRAMER
1864-1947

FLORENCE E.
KRAMER
1887-1943

HAZEL M.
KRAMER
BAGBY
1889-1964

FRANCIS
BAGBY
1886-1946

JOHN BAGBY
1918-2005

WALKER BAGBY
1924-2010

SON   CYNTHIA
BAGBY

SON   NANCY
BAGBY

Kramer-White-Bagby Family Tree

The Story Waiting to be Told

My father had a secret that he believed needed keeping.

As best he could, he kept the details of it from my mother throughout their marriage, offering only a skeleton-truth for her to flesh out in some way that she could accept and live with. To my sister and me, he gave no hint at all. Everything I knew of my father's life occurred either when he was a child or after he met my mother. The decades of the 1930s and '40s were empty. I knew nothing of them.

My parents were married in 1955, both considerably older than the average newlyweds of the time. My father was 46 years old, and my mother, 34. Dad had grown up in a poor, fiercely political family in Wisconsin that held tight to its Irish roots, and my mother was raised by my grandmother in a small Alabama town. Her family had been well-off and prominent until her father died in 1928, leaving my grandmother to raise four children at the brink of the Great Depression. By the time my parents met in Washington, D.C., both assumed that they might never be fortunate enough to have children. That I was born a year-and-a-half later was viewed as extraordinary good luck. When my sister, Terri, was born four years after that, when they were 40 and 52, they saw it as nothing short of a miracle. We lived a charmed life in Arlington, Virginia, until we lost my father in December of 1973.

In the sad months that followed losing him, I often peppered my mother with questions about the past, seeking to learn as much as I could about this man who had been taken away from me too soon. I was seventeen when she spilled to me what she took to be a great scandal. That day she leaned close to me, and in a hushed voice, her soft drawl even softer than it normally was, said:

"Your Daddy was married before he married me. For quite a while."

I was astonished. "What? When? For how long?"

"He met her when they were both at the University of Wisconsin. They got married back then. In the 1930s sometime. I think they were married for about fifteen years."

Fifteen years! That was a very long time. "Did they have children?" I asked her. I immediately began to fantasize about the long lost brother or sister I had out there somewhere in the world.

"No," my mother said. "No children."

"What happened to her?"

My mother's voice dropped even lower. "She died."

I could tell from her tone that this was no ordinary death. "How?"

"I don't know exactly. Your Daddy never wanted to talk about it. But they weren't living together when she died... She was somewhere—I don't know—somewhere foreign, I think." Her voice fell to a whisper. "I think there was another man with her at the time."

"Oh my God!"

"Don't take the Lord's name," my mother replied automatically.

"But how exactly did she die?"

"I don't know. I think it was something maybe about her heart?"

"Didn't you ask Daddy what happened?"

"I told you. He didn't like to talk about it."

"Well, don't you know anything else?"

She paused, and then offered, "Her name was Hazel Kramer."

"Hazel!" I said. "The same name as you!"

Mama smiled. "Yes, your Daddy didn't like it one bit when he found out that was my name. He didn't like to remember her."

"So—is that all?" I pushed. "All that you know?"

"Well, I know that she used to be Tennessee Williams' girlfriend."

If the top of my head could have come off from sheer astonishment, that would have been the moment.

*   *   *

My father and I only talked about Tennessee Williams once that I can remember. It was September 1973, a hot Virginia night where the only cool air to be found came from the box fan that whirred by the sofa where my father sat with his Manhattan and the evening paper. It was one of the last weeks that I had with him before he went into the hospital for what should have been a simple, straightforward operation, but did not turn out that way. In several months, he would be dead.

That particular evening, as always, he wanted to know what I was studying in school. My father was deaf, and he wore a hearing aid, a device that seemed to me then a useless bit of plastic that often became dislodged from his ear, splitting the air with a piercing and frequently embarrassing whistle. It didn't seem to be of any use in helping him to hear us. That night, as every night, I would have had to rely on careful enunciations that he could lip-read and laborious fingerspelling and hand signals.

I hurried through the math, Spanish and history, and then added, "In English, we're reading *The Glass Menagerie*."

How hard must it have been for him to hear that and to say nothing? To not take advantage of that moment to impress me by remarking casually, *Oh, yes, I knew Tom Williams.* My father, who craved fame and revered writers, must certainly have considered for a moment telling me at least a little of what he knew.

Instead, he said only, "That's a good play. Do you like it?"

And so I never got to hear him tell me the story that was his to tell. That story was then locked in a steamer trunk in our basement, the contents of which not even my mother had seen. Indeed, she had vowed never to open it, a vow that she would one day break. Had I known where to look, much of the story waited in the file drawers that held my father's unpublished plays, short fiction, and longer works.

But I didn't know then that there was any story worth seeking. It's true that in 1975, when Williams' book *Memoirs* was published, I eagerly thumbed through the index in the bookstore, looking for my father's name. And there he was, Terrence McCabe, on page 38:

> The onset of my cardiovascular condition occurred in the spring of 1934, and [...] was triggered by two things. First, the quite unexpected marriage of Hazel to a young man named Terrence McCabe, whom she had been dating at the University of Wisconsin. I felt as though the sky had fallen on me, and my reaction was to start working every evening on short stories, overcoming fatigue with black coffee.
>
> One evening I was at work on a story titled "The Accent of a Coming Foot" [...] I had arrived at a climactic scene when I suddenly became aware that my heart was palpitating and skipping beats.[1]

I showed it to my mother. She read through the pages in which he went on to describe his episode with his heart, and how he ended up in the cardiac ward at St. Vincent's Hospital for ten days.

My mother had a sharply defined sense of propriety and believed it to be a sign of good breeding to attract as little attention to oneself as possible. I'm sure that this statement by Williams in a best-selling book embarrassed her. When she read it, she wrinkled her nose disdainfully. "Oh, I don't like this at all. He's saying that your Daddy gave him a heart attack."

It would be many years before I understood that what Williams was likely experiencing was closer to an anxiety attack, and that there was no indication whatsoever that Williams blamed my father for the situation. And it would be many more before I caught the factual errors in his story. My father and Hazel Kramer married in 1935, not 1934. And it was not in the spring, but in September.

All I cared about back then was that my father was famous. If he had caused the renowned Tennessee Williams to have a heart attack, then that was a story with teeth in it. I told it often, loving the reaction I could elicit from my listeners. As the years went by, and I became a high school teacher, I took great pleasure in regaling my students with my connection, however peripheral, to Tennessee Williams' past. It made a good story. And I love a good story. I didn't yet know that the story I knew was merely a fragment of what there was to tell.

*   *   *

When I was fifteen, Dad gave me an unsolicited piece of advice that I have never forgotten, so vehemently was it imparted. That I could have done anything to merit it seems unlikely, as my experience of the opposite sex at that time in my life was—much to my sorrow—severely limited.

We were sitting together on the living room sofa, and he looked me straight in the eye and shook his I'm-teaching-you-a-valuable-lesson finger at me.

"Always," he said, and then repeated for emphasis. "Always be a lady."

I laughed. "How do I do that?"

He leaned in closer, and he didn't smile back. "You want to know how to be a lady? Watch your mother. *That's* a lady. You couldn't have a better example."

I nodded, though from my perspective, such a role model didn't allow for much in the way of fun over the rest of my long, dull, ladylike life.

"So, who's someone who's *not* a lady?"

He waved his hand dismissively. "Don't you worry about that. There are plenty of 'em. You just act like your mother. Your mother would never do anything she had to be ashamed of."

He settled back and picked up his newspaper, but I could tell he was still agitated by whatever had motivated this shared wisdom.

If my father looked at my mother—a quiet magnolia-blossom of a woman from a small Alabama town, who, as far as I could see, had never committed a sin in all of her unimpeachable life—and then held her up to me as the light I should hold aloft as I moved into the future, what would he have thought of my secrets? What would he have made of his firstborn had he lived to see me grow up?

He died when I was just sixteen. I had then been kissed by only three boys and that had been the extent of my romantic history. As a college freshman, I set out to undo the good-girl reputation I'd had in childhood as swiftly as I possibly could. Fueled by the encouragement of magazines like *Cosmopolitan* that were then riding the wave of the sexual revolution, I felt wild and unleashed after years spent under the eye of my watchful mother. Would my father have forgiven me for the wild, smoke-and-beer-blurred ride I had taken through the late '70s? The boys whose names I have forgotten? And later, the marriages that creaked and broke beneath the weight of bad decisions? Would my father have disowned me as one of the fallen, the women who were not ladies, who blackened their good names and could never undo the deed? Or would my father have come to accept the woman that I became?

*　　　　*　　　　*

I began my quest to learn about the story of my father, the first Hazel, and Tennessee Williams in May 2013. A close friend sent me an email with an offhand question that so intrigued me that it set me on a course to uncover the story that I had not known existed. He asked me, "Did you know that, in his later years, Tennessee Williams wrote a play called *The Red Devil Battery Sign* in which there is a character actually named Terrence McCabe?"

I had not known. But I was about to find out. About that, and more.

The year leading up to the onset of my preoccupation with my father's former life had been a difficult and unsettling one for me. My marriage had buckled under the weight of a revelation I found I could not live with. Although I tried hard to keep that union together, it fell apart with a suddenness that left me reeling. This was not my first marital failure, and I felt particularly hard-hit to know that, yet again, I had made a commitment that I would not be able to keep. The breakup forced me to move from the familiar home I had lived in since I was twenty-seven. In the year that followed these losses, my mother died after a long and memory-devastating illness, and my beloved sister, Terri, named for our father, was diagnosed with cancer.

Nothing seemed predictable or certain. The future was a slippery thing that could slide from my grasp in an instant. But the past was something that could not be changed. I might never know it fully. I might have to search relentlessly to uncover the life my father had lived before he married my mother and to reveal the woman he had so deeply loved when he was a young man. But the story was real. It had an essential truth to it that could not be altered, if only I would look deeply enough.

At the time I received my friend's email, many of my possessions were still in boxes, and I began to dig through them, looking for the artifacts of my father's life that I had somehow managed to claim for myself when my mother moved from my childhood home. I remembered a black and moldering album of photos and clippings. I had thought that the album was my father's, but when at last I came upon it again as I searched for clues, I realized with a start that the album had actually belonged to Hazel. Here were not only photographs of her mother, her grandparents and my father, but also a to-do list scrawled on a tattered yellow paper of tasks to be accomplished before their wedding, newspaper clippings announcing their engagement and a hotel's "Do Not Disturb" sign—a testament to a moment so intimate and yet so naively young and hopeful that it made my heart ache for both of them.

I looked through all the photos I found of them when they were young and in love. One shows Hazel sitting on my father's lap, smiling, almost laughing, directly into the camera, one hand resting on my father's chest, the other around his neck. My father looks up at her with what can only be called adoration, a grin on his face, his eyes fixed on hers.

I have never seen a single photograph of my mother sitting on my father's lap.

They look so blissful, so unaware of all that will happen later. Perhaps she went on to do terrible things to my father. Perhaps he did a terrible thing or two himself. But seeing them like this, I just couldn't believe it. And I found welling up in me a kind of pity, a tenderness for this as yet undefiled love. I have known this place. I have felt that stubborn hope that rises in the heart and spirit when one feels that real and enduring love has been found at last. What a grace it is that none of us know at the time that it will all be taken away, that what is surely love can be so thoroughly lost and ruined.

I found also a series of photographs that they clearly took of each other, experimenting with lighting. In several, she is lying back on a couch or bed, in what is so blatantly an effort to look alluring, seductive, that it made me embarrassed for her. She is not a classically pretty woman, but in each of these shots, a heat rises up from her, a languorous desire to be seen, to be admired, to be touched.

In one of the photos in this series, she even appears to be naked, though perhaps the top of her low-cut dress is simply out of the frame. And yet, I believe she would have easily posed naked for my father. And I can also imagine what happened after they grew restless with taking pictures.

I have never seen photographs like this of my mother.

In another photo, Hazel Kramer is a songbird. A torch singer. She stands with her arms held away from her body. Her chin is lifted, her white skin made even whiter by whatever light there is in the room. The enormous brown eyes watch me. Her mouth opens to release a note.

There is a caption below the photo: "The thrills and frills of nightclub life are gaining favor with University of Wisconsin students this fall, and here is one of the reasons. She is Miss Hazel Kramer, co-ed from St. Louis, shown here in one of the Mae West numbers she enacts as a featured entertainer in the floor shows at the 770 Club."

The year is 1933. Two Mae West films were released that year: *She Done Him Wrong* and *I'm No Angel*, both with Cary Grant. They were the last of West's films released before the censors clamped down on all the risqué wordplay, the suggestive lyrics. I wonder which song she is singing here. Something sweet and romantic, perhaps, like "I Want You, I Need You"? No. I don't think so. This is a Mae West revue, after all, and Mae West is known not for her sweetness, but for her sass. For her bawdiness. I turn back to the photo and put other West lyrics into Hazel's mouth:

Aw, come on, let me cling on to ya like a vine
Make that lowdown music trickle off your spine

Baby, I can warm ya with this love of mine
I'm no angel...

Why choose to sing Mae West if you are not going to play it up, sex it up, and wait for the whoops and whistles?

For a moment, I think back to one of my earliest memories of my mother. She is in the kitchen, washing the dinner dishes before leaving for her weekly choir practice at our church. Her flawless soprano, careful and sweet, fills every room in the house. *O Lord my God, when I in awesome wonder, consider all the worlds thy hands have made...*

In that photo of Hazel, my father is at the piano. The caption continues, *She is accompanied here by Terrence McCabe, campus pianist.*

Campus pianist! Once upon a time, it seems, my father could play music. He could hear music, the deafness he was born with in one ear not yet having found its way into the other. He is all profile and chiseled cheekbone here, handsome in a way that startles me. Here he is not my father. I can understand why she wants him.

After finding Hazel's photo album, I began to search in earnest for the full story behind my father's former life. One of the first revelations came, fittingly enough, from Tennessee Williams himself. In a *Playboy* interview that ran in April of 1973, Williams spoke briefly of Hazel, and the similarities they shared later in life: "Hazel and I both went on pills and liquor. She married another man but killed herself when she was still very young."[2]

Suicide. This is not the story my mother was told.

Did my father see this interview? It appeared five months before he entered the hospital, eight months before he died. Certainly if he had seen the issue on a newsstand in our local drugstore, with cover copy advertising an interview with Tennessee Williams, he would have been curious to know what Tom had had to say.

As I continued to search through Hazel's album and papers, I made another startling discovery. Deep in the bottom of a large envelope that also contained a greeting card and several small photographs, I found a newspaper notice of Hazel's death. Four words leapt out at me: "suddenly, in Mexico City." Was "suddenly" a euphemism for what had really occurred? A couple of people, when questioned, had mentioned that they had heard she had died in a car accident. Was the accident a story my father had fabricated to hide the truth? If she had killed herself, why had she done so?

I didn't know it yet, but this question would haunt me over the course of several years of research and searching.

In another album, I have a snapshot that was taken of me as an infant. On the back of it my father has scrawled a message, no doubt to his own parents. It reads: *Whatever my sins, real or imagined, this little girl has absolved them for me.* The first time I had ever read those words, I smiled. It showed me how deeply my father had loved me. But now I revisited the message, and read it differently. What were the sins that needed absolving? Had my father merely imagined some wrongdoing, perhaps out of guilt, or had he actually done something wrong, something of which he was deeply ashamed?

*   *   *

I went looking for the story of how Hazel died, and I found it. Or found parts of it. Enough pieces to fit together to realize that there were pieces missing, pieces that would make all the difference in understanding exactly what had happened, not only to her, but to my father.

My mother had told me she believed there may have been another man with Hazel when she died. And there had been; a man who discovered her body after she had succumbed to an overdose of Seconals. A man who told police that he had been given a key to her apartment in *el distrito federal* so that he might check on her, concerned because she drank heavily and took sleeping pills. A man who had checked on her twice that day, before finally finding her dead the third time that he checked. A man with a wife of his own. An American man who said he had known her several years before, when they both lived in New York City. A man with a name that was common enough that finding him would prove very difficult.

When I first began searching for information about Hazel and about my father's marriage to her, I had no way of knowing that this curiosity would grow into a full-scale investigation that would consume me for two years. The answers did not come easily. The facts and leads I began to uncover led to still more questions that complicated the mystery. As I began to realize how much I did not know about my father's life, a fire was lit in me that I could not put out. The desire to know propelled me forward. I knew that what I discovered might forever alter my view of my father. But what mattered to me most was that I have a chance to know him more completely than our years together had allowed. And, surprisingly, as I continued my search, what also became important to me was Hazel herself. Her story was a complicated one, fraught with sadness, loss, and loneliness. Something in that story called to me. Perhaps it was simply the indignity of her apparent disappearance from history. She had lived a life full of dreams and ambitions and loves, as we all do. But no one remained to speak for her, to lift her name to the light. I was an unlikely prospect for that job. Yet, without planning it, it was a job I took on anyway.

As I began to investigate her death, I learned that Mexico City is not a place known for its careful record keeping. I tried first to employ two separate Mexican private investigators, but both refused to take my job. The man I sought had been questioned by police and then released. I was told that in Mexico, no records would have been kept unless there had been an actual conviction. And even then, sixty-two years had passed since that night. I was searching for one small grain of sand along a beach covered by billions of such grains. They shrugged, said no, and wished me *buena suerte*. I was left to my own ingenuity.

Every night I would Google his name, Sam Bern, along with other key words that might single him out among the countless hits that would turn up and lead me nowhere. I encountered a young man with the same name who suffered from a debilitating illness. I found another man with that name who was a noted outdoorsman. I searched his full name; I searched possible nicknames. I made a family tree for him on Ancestry. com and found yet another gentleman with that name who had also lived in New York City, but was born twenty years too early to be my guy.

It was nearing the end of the summer, and I was growing desperate. I would return to my teaching job in just a week, and I knew that then my time to devote to researching would be severely limited. It was well after midnight and I tried yet another search, expecting to encounter the same fruitless links and wrong paths that I had combed through all August.

But this time there was something different: an announcement for a wedding that had taken place in 2009. The groom's grandfather, referred to as deceased, was Sam Bern. Something about this hit felt unlike all the others. I felt a thrill of possibility. The groom had an even more common name than his grandfather, but I knew the city he was living in. I searched for him on Facebook, and bingo. I scrolled through his friend list. There was a woman there who was a generation older, the mother or aunt of the groom, with the last name "Bern." I sent messages to both of them. To the woman, I said that I was looking for this man who had once lived in Mexico City, and wondered if, perhaps, she was his daughter.

A week later, a message from her: "Yes," she wrote me. "That sounds like my father."

What followed over the next few months was a clumsy "court-ship," like so many courtships that I would enter into in the next two years, in which I tried to get her to open up and talk to me. Ultimately, she told me very little. The most startling piece of information she shared was that her mother, a woman named Loretta, Sam Bern's wife, was still alive. She was 94, remarried and living in Florida.

The daughter questioned Loretta and told me that her mother remembered nothing of Hazel or her unfortunate death. I tried writing to Loretta directly, sending photographs of Hazel that I hoped might jar her memory. I received no reply.

What did the silence mean? I considered several possibilities. Perhaps Loretta truly had no memory at all of Hazel or of that fateful night in Mexico City. Maybe her husband had lied when he told the police that both he and his wife were friends of Hazel's; maybe it was only he who had known her; maybe he had hidden this relationship from his wife. Or perhaps Loretta remembered all too well, and did not want to relive the past – or did not want her daughter to learn unpleasant truths about her father.

These are the kind of dead ends that I have encountered, time and again, in trying to understand what happened in my father's first marriage. This search to learn more about the man who was with Hazel the night she died—a search that is still ongoing—is only one small facet of the quest that has driven me since I began this research into my father's first marriage. Two years have passed, and what I have unearthed has been considerable. I have read virtually every book available, either by or about Tennessee Williams. I have read, as well, the Williams works that include characters modeled on either Hazel or my father. I have discovered my father's own book about that marriage, a thinly veiled memoir disguised as a novel. I contacted a cousin who had known Hazel and searched for and found the daughter of my father's best friend, who remembered Hazel from the days when she was a teenager. I have tracked down three court cases filed by Hazel in a dispute involving her grandmother's will, traveling to Chicago to research two of those cases, and stumbling upon the testimony of my own grandparents. I contacted the daughter of Esmeralda Mayes, a close childhood friend of both Hazel and Tom, and enlisted her help in searching through her mother's papers for information about Hazel. I searched for, and found, the grandchildren of Hazel's biological father.

A friend joked that I have become a "stalker." If it is possible to stalk a ghost, then I concede that it may be true. I have even dreamed about her, which is not surprising, for I have spent entire days sifting through her life, as well as the lives of those who knew her. At night, when I lie in bed trying to unwind and sleep, my mind will not always let go of her. I petition her in the darkness; I try to bargain with her in a manner that is almost like a prayer. *Let me tell your story*, I say to her. *Let me undo your death.*

A Character Named Terrence McCabe

Pierce Brosnan created the role of my father.

Williams' play *The Red Devil Battery Sign* opened June 18, 1975, in Boston, but despite generally favorable notices, closed after only a week. Williams decided that the play's controversial political themes were too explosive for American audiences at that time and elected to have the play reopen in London. Williams selected a very young Pierce Brosnan to play the part of Terrence McCabe, and according to reviews, Brosnan garnered much favorable attention for his portrayal of the young Irishman. In fact, Brosnan still has the telegram Williams sent him after the opening, which read, "Thank God for you, dear boy."[3]

My father would have loved to know that an actor as stunningly good-looking as Brosnan had been chosen personally by Tom to play the part of Terry McCabe. My father considered himself an unattractive man. In a short autobiography that he had composed while he was still in his thirties, Dad had written about his adolescent self: "Because of his size and homely countenance, he was more of a boy's boy than a youthful Casanova."[4] In another book that he wrote about his youth in Superior, Wisconsin, he mentions that people, upon meeting him, often remarked "how much I resembled my father... I duly noted that the verb was 'resembled' and not 'look like'; my father was a good-looking man, which explains that."[5] My grandfather was indeed a handsome man, and my father compared his own appearance against that standard and found himself wanting.

My father's lifelong sensitivity about his looks would have an impact on me as well, as I grew out of childhood and into my teen years. I knew from reading letters that he had written to his parents while I was a baby that he thought me quite pretty; he remarked on this often and with clear delight. But early adolescence was not especially kind to me. I had inherited not only Dad's dark eyes and hair, but also his thin face and large nose. My skin began to break out. And in the 8th grade, I was prescribed glasses for my nearsightedness.

I spent a long time in the optometrist's shop while my mother waited, hoping to pick out just the right frames. I ultimately selected gold wire-rim, which I thought looked nice on me. But that evening, when Dad came home and I modeled the glasses for him, he seemed not nearly as enchanted by them as I had been. I later heard him say to my mother, "No boy will ever look at her now."

I was crushed by this. My excitement about the new pair of glasses was gone in an instant, and I made every effort at school to avoid wearing them. Whenever possible, I sat near the front of the classroom. And when forced into a back row, I perfected the trick of holding one lens of the glasses up to an eye like a monocle, just long enough to make out whatever I needed to read on the blackboard.

Yet I never for a moment believed—nor do I now—that my father was being deliberately cruel when he made that remark to my mother. I understood even then that he hoped for me a happier adolescence than the one he had suffered through. He loved me and wanted to protect me from the pain of being excluded or ignored.

And so when I read about the stunningly handsome Pierce Brosnan creating the role of Terry McCabe, I was thrilled on my father's behalf. Dad may not have seen himself as an attractive ladies' man, but apparently Tom Williams had.

It's not so difficult to find out what Williams thought of Hazel. He called her his "great female love."[6] She was "a redhead with great liquid brown eyes and a skin of pearly translucence."[7] But there is less to find on Tennessee Williams' thoughts about my father. Lyle Leverich's well-respected study of Williams' early years, called simply *Tom*, recounts the moment when Tom learned that Hazel was engaged to my father and a later meeting between them:

> On an occasion when Miss Florence was giving one of her impromptu recitals at Edwina's piano, she suddenly stopped and announced that Hazel was engaged to be married in September to someone she had met in Wisconsin. His name was Terrence McCabe.
>
> Characteristically, Tom gave no outward sign of his feelings. Years later, however, Tennessee admitted that Terry "was a personable young Irishman of fantastic humor, and we hit it off well. I recall an hilarious evening the three of us spent together, after getting quite drunk—at least I did at the St. Louis Athletic Club. We drove around town, singing and exchanging mad jokes." But such "an hilarious evening" must always end sadly when "the three of us" became the two of them and the one of him. Regarding Hazel, he confessed, "I never loved anyone as I loved her," and long after she married McCabe, Tennessee told his mother that the beautiful redhead was very much the deepest love of his life.[8]

Williams concedes that my father was "personable," good natured and full of fun, all things I know to be true. I can't help but note that Williams doesn't seem to resent my father personally. He just seems heartbroken.

Dakin Williams wrote a book about his brother Tom called *His Brother's Keeper* that sheds even more light on Tom's reaction to meeting my father. The first time I hurried to the pages that contained references to Terrence McCabe, I found myself actually laughing out loud at Dakin's description of Dad:

> [The Williams and Kramer families] found that Terry McCabe was about as different as possible from Tom, a tall, thin, extroverted, backslapping fellow who was the life of the party.
>
> Tom, quiet, shy, introverted and heartbroken, listened as Terry told a joke that Dakin still remembers as the only thing he can recall clearly about McCabe.
>
> "Did you hear this one about the stockbroker?" said Terry. "He was telling his new client, 'Hold your gas, let your water go, sit on your American Can! Scott tissues went down three points. Thousands were wiped clean!'" Great guffaws from Miss Florence."[9]

It must be said that corny jokes such as this one were a staple of my childhood. I could picture my father telling this joke because I had seen him tell so many others like it. And I also knew instantly that what Dakin took to be extroversion was anything but. Instead, Dad's animation and "back-slapping" was actually an elaborately orchestrated defense he had contrived to deal with both his insecurities and his deafness. Dad had learned as his hearing gradually worsened that his handicap was less noticeable if *he* was the one in charge of the conversation. And thus, he was always the instigator, the speaker, the storyteller. He tried to prevent situations where others would ask him questions and he would need to be the one who responded, for then his hearing loss might become a problem that others noticed. He tried to avoid those moments at all costs.

I realized something else as I read Dakin's account of this meeting. Certainly Hazel must have told Dad many stories about her family before their St. Louis trip, and very likely, had let him know all about her grandfather being an avid trader in the stock market. And because of this, I've no doubt that Dad must have planned this particular ice-breaking joke days ahead of their meeting. He had probably practiced it more than once, perhaps looking into his own reflection in the mirror as he shaved that morning. He had wanted very much to make a good impression, to make the Kramers like him. His vulnerability broke my heart.

While I knew this account must be true, Dakin also added a good deal of other, frankly cryptic, information: "Tom never asked another woman to marry him. Hazel's marriage ended in tragedy. She broke up with Terry years later, and this affected Miss Florence so much that she committed suicide."

I would later learn that Miss Florence had not committed suicide; where Dakin got this idea is beyond me. As for the other revelations, back then I could only wonder: What sort of tragedy had ended the marriage? Did he mean Hazel's death, or had the marriage ended before that event?

It would be a while before I had anything approaching a satisfying answer to these questions.

*   *   *

In the months after I discovered its presence in my home, I would spend untold evening hours with Hazel's old photo album. I had to turn the pages gingerly. The paper crumbled and flaked at my touch, leaving dark tatters across the cream-colored carpet. The tips of my fingers turned black and dusty.

Most of the photographs were glued into place, or attached with large, rusting staples. I wanted to peek at the backs of them to see if I could find names, dates, but I was afraid of ripping them. Nonetheless, because of the reading I had begun to do about Hazel's early life, I could identify the members of the Kramer family. Her grandparents, Emil and Emma, who had adopted her, seemed a dour pair. I found only one photograph in which Emma was smiling, and then it was only a half-smile.

Hazel's mother, however, seemed to smile often. Florence had a broad, coarse face, a short, round body, and looked to me nothing at all like her tall, seemingly elegant daughter. Williams' mother, Edwina, thought Florence common, his brother Dakin called her flamboyant, and Williams himself referred to her as "an antic butterball."[10]

I found a photo of Dad and Hazel beneath a large shade tree, both with catcher's mitts on their hands, and Dad sporting a base-ball cap. Hazel's face is playful, amused. I suddenly recalled my own days of playground shame, swinging wildly at approaching balls, the bat whacking against nothing but the gnat-infested air. Dad would take me down to the vacant lot after supper, school-ing me with soft, underhanded pitches and instructions on how to stand, how to angle my body so that bat could connect with ball. I imagined Dad counseling Hazel the way he had counseled me, pictured her laughing and swinging. Missing, and not really caring.

Though perhaps she was more of a tomboy than I ever was. On one page of the album, Hazel had glued gift tags from their various holidays together. One read, "A lily would be a reflec-tion on such a toughy —so it is roses for my roughneck on our first Easter." At the very least, then, she had put on a veneer of toughness. Another tag that was also in my father's handwriting read simply, "One-twelfth of our first anniversary together and no fights yet." I smiled at this. How young, hopeful, and sweet it was that they had given each other anniversary presents for every month of their first year together. On one of the tags Hazel had written this message: "To my husband, who was, is, and will always be my Valentine." What had happened, I wondered, to change this early devotion?

I thought of the men I had written similar messages to over my lifetime. "Always" so often turned out to be a much shorter time than I had expected it would be. I had entered into several marriages that failed. With each, I had been so full of hope, so determined to make the union last. The failures of these marriages gradually whittled away at the "happily-ever-after" ideal I had clung to throughout my childhood and adolescence. By the time I discovered Hazel's album, I had made a vow to myself never to marry again.

Nonetheless, I did not plan to swear off a loving and committed relationship. I met my current partner, Chris, in late 2011, and over many months, we grew very close. He did not share my reluctance to marry again, but he accepted it. And because he shares custody of his son and wishes to be close to him, our relationship has been confined primarily to weekends, and this has worked out well for us both over the last five years.

And so Chris came over on the weekend, laden with books from the library where he worked. He brought me Tennessee Williams' *Notebooks*, both volumes of his *Selected Letters*, a collection of interviews called *Conversations with Tennessee Williams,* and a copy of the play *The Red Devil Battery Sign*. Together we combed through the indices and pages looking for mention of Hazel and my father.

"Come upstairs and look through the photo album with me," I said. "I want to show you what I've found."

I opened the album, its seams already coming loose, and carefully turned each page. At the bottom of one page was a photograph I had not noticed before. Chris put his hand on my arm, stopping me from turning to the next leaf in the album.

"Wait," he said, leaning closer to look at the photo of a young man seated in a chair. "Is that...?"

His voice trailed off, and I looked down to study the photograph more intently. The dark hair, the shape of the face, the turn of the smile seemed familiar from all of the books about Williams that I had been reading.

"Oh my God," I said. "Do you think it could be?"

"Yes," he said, leaning in next to me. "I think it's Williams."

The photo was not in good condition. Even at the time it had been taken, it would have been a somewhat blurry image. But time had faded the ink, rendering the hazy image in a sepia tone. And yet—it looked very much like this might be a young Tom Williams, perhaps in his early twenties.

Gently and painstakingly slowly, I worked to loosen the glue and tape that held the photograph in place. I needed verification that this was indeed Tennessee Williams. Somehow, I would find someone who would know.

*　　　　*　　　　*

Through the remainder of May and into June, I kept up the semblance of living in 2013. I got up each morning and drove into school; I planned for and taught my classes; I administered final exams. But just below the surface of the self I presented each day to the world, my thoughts moved constantly through a different landscape. Here my father was still alive: young, handsome, hopeful, in a way that I had never known him before. Hazel was here, too: no longer the immobile woman with enormous eyes who looked blankly out of all the photographs I had found, but a young girl who still believed that her life might turn out exactly as she hoped it would.

I knew that girl. Once I had been that girl, too.

They kept me company through all of my waking hours, and remained with me while I dreamed. Many mornings I awoke with some new idea of where to search for signs of them, as if they had whispered directions to me while I was sleeping. Each new discovery made them clearer, and yet each created even more questions.

Every time I searched, it seemed I turned up more clues that led me somewhere I had not yet been. In one of my many searches for connections between my father and Tennessee Williams, I found a link to a book called *Tennessee Williams: A Literary Life* by John Bak, a well-respected authority on Williams. He had written a number of things about my father, but one mention especially intrigued me: "Hazel eventually enrolled at the University of Wisconsin, where she would meet, and later marry, Terrence McCabe, whom Williams would immortalize in name and evil deed in the play *Battle of Angels* a little over a decade later."[11]

This was surprising. I knew about the character in *The Red Devil Battery Sign,* but could it be possible there was another Williams character named Terrence McCabe? I searched through my collections of Williams' plays and studied the cast list for *Battle of Angels.* I found no character with my father's name. I looked again. This time I noticed a character named Jabe Torrance.

Just as the character Terrence McCabe in *The Red Devil Battery Sign* was an antagonist, so, too, was Jabe. Though he doesn't appear onstage until the very end of the play, he makes his unpleasant presence known throughout the story by rapping imperiously on the floor with his cane in an effort to get his wife, Myra, to wait on him. He is an invalid, dying of cancer, in an upstairs bedroom, and Myra, unhappy and unfulfilled, is tied to him only by obligation. Was this Williams' commentary on the choice Hazel had made in marrying my father?

I searched for a way to contact John Bak and finally located him in France at the University of Lorraine. He responded to my email within a day, no doubt surprised to hear who I was. In response to my question about the characters in *Battle of Angels* and *The Red Devil Battery Sign*, he wrote: "Yes, Terrence McCabe is a character in *Red Devil*, and honestly, I should have mentioned that play more than *Battle*. It is only apocrypha that he played with your father's name for the villain Jabe Torrance in *Battle*."[12]

Apocryphal, perhaps, but the suppositions rose out of somewhere, and to me, the name seemed too close to Dad's to be mere chance.

I also mentioned to him the photograph that might possibly be of young Tom. He asked that I scan it and send it to him. All at once, knowing that expert eyes were going to peruse it, the photograph suddenly seemed less like Williams than I had previously thought.

His answer came back almost immediately: "I'm 95 percent certain that that is indeed Williams in the photo. It is a bit blurry, but it is him."[13]

He went on to suggest that I write to Robert Bray, the editor of *The Tennessee Williams Review*, and share the photograph with him, as well.

Bray wrote me back: "Yes, the photo is certainly Tom Williams."[14]

I had also shared with Bray that I had known about my father's marriage to Hazel since Dad's death in 1973, and his response to this intrigued me.

"The whole Hazel Kramer story is very sad," he said. "I'm sorry you have had to live with this revelation since 1973."[15]

What did he mean, very sad? What did he know that I did not? I wrote back to ask him to elaborate. He told me only that he had heard Hazel committed suicide, and that he knew nothing beyond that.

*   *   *

As I read through Williams' *Notebooks*, I learned what a common thing it was for him to use the names of family and friends in his plays, and also how many of his poems and short stories were also either inspired by or based on people from his life.

Scholar Margaret Bradham Thornton provides copious notes throughout Williams' reproduced journal text that illuminated a lot for me, about my father and many others.

In a journal entry from September 15, 1937, Tom writes, "Saw Miss Flo tonight—she is displeased with Terry."[16] In a helpful textual note to the left of this remark, Thornton writes:

> Terrence McCabe married Hazel Kramer in September 1935. In the 1970s play, *The Red Devil Battery Sign*, Williams would give the married boyfriend of King Del Rey's daughter the name of Terrence McCabe. King, upset that his daughter is unmarried and pregnant, blames McCabe (act 3, scene 1):
> "Such a lovely Irish name. You run out of potatoes too fucking quick and you come here too many and you decided it wasn't potatoes you wanted but liquor and parades and wakes and political power. Bosses and corruption. Oh, back home you're into revolution but here you're into—ripoff... Christ, you babyface mother!"[17]

Reading this, I was sure that when I began reading *Red Devil* that my father would come across as the most despicable villain ever to darken a page, and yet in a much later journal entry, from 1979, Williams discusses his homosexuality, and writes of my father in a markedly different tone: "I could have been passably 'normal'—(I loved Hazel Kramer from the age of eleven till she married a likeable Irishman at the University of Wisconsin. Now both of them are dead)."[18]

Two things struck me about this short statement: the first being that Tom, for all that he may have resented Dad and felt angry and hurt about his presence in Hazel's life, had liked my father. I am as sure as I have ever been of anything that my father, knowing how Tom felt about Hazel, would have tried very hard to ingratiate himself with this spurned suitor, that he would have been as charming, witty, and kind as I knew him capable of being. The second realization was that Williams had somehow learned of my father's death in 1973. I couldn't know if the two of them had kept up through the years, or if Williams had stumbled upon this news accidentally.

I also learned of all the other people in Williams' life whose names or memory had been appropriated for his vast output of plays, short stories, and poems. First and foremost would be his sister, Rose. They had been as close as twins while growing up, but the situation began to change when Rose hit adolescence; she began to exhibit strange behaviors, irrational fears and violent outbursts, and these increased as time went by. She was diagnosed with "dementia praecox"—the term in vogue at the time for schizophrenia—and ultimately would be lobotomized in 1943, a tragedy that forever altered her hope of a normal life.

Thornton writes that Rose would be "the model for more than fifteen characters," but certainly the most famous of these was the painfully shy, socially anxious Laura in *The Glass Menagerie*. Aspects of Rose also appear in Blanche in *A Streetcar Named Desire*, Alma in *Summer and Smoke*, Hannah in *The Night of the Iguana*, and Clare in *The Two-Character Play*, to name just a few of the more-well known plays. Williams included Rose-inspired characters in numerous short stories as well, and wrote poems about her. Moreover, he included mentions of lobotomies and mental illness in quite a number of works.

Some of the other people from Williams' life who have ended up depicted in his work are Hazel's grandparents, Emil and Emma Kramer; her mother, Florence; his maternal grandmother; his father, Cornelius; his mother, Edwina; and his good friend, Esmeralda Mayes. Even acquaintances might have discovered themselves immortalized, as was Jim Connor, whose name was used for the Gentleman Caller in *The Glass Menagerie*, and Harold Mitchell and Stanley Kowalski, who both ended up as characters in *A Streetcar Named Desire*.[19]

Hazel also inspired a wealth of material. In a journal entry on March 9, 1936, about six months after Hazel's marriage to Dad, Tom writes of seeing her on one of her many trips home to visit her mother. "Saw H.B. and was inspired to write a poem by certain lines in her face...Visited Jewel Box with H.B. and M.F."[20] Thornton provides the following notes about this entry:

> H.B. is presumably Hazel Elizabeth (Beth) Kramer... Williams may have chosen to refer to Hazel as "H.B." since he was disappointed by her marriage to another man and may not have wanted to refer to her by her married name. Two early poems make reference to a young girl's face, "Lyric" and "The Mystery of Your Smile."...
>
> M.F. is presumably Miss Florence, Hazel Kramer's mother. Williams often went to Forest Park with the Kramers.[21]

Thornton provides the text of the two poems she mentions in her note, and it seems probable that both were written for Hazel. Neither is an especially good poem, but the one that appears to me the likelier candidate between the two is "The Mystery Of Your Smile:" "If only I had power to know / The secrets of your smile-- / To tell how much is tenderness / And how much simply guile!"[22]

In his autobiography, *Memoirs*, Williams also notes that one of the characters in his story, "Three Players Of a Summer Game" is modeled on Hazel as a young girl.[23] It is also widely accepted that his failed romantic relationship with her was what inspired the short stories "The Accent of a Coming Foot" and "The Field of Blue Children," as well as the play "April Is the Cruelest Month," revised as *Spring Storm*.[24] Characters modeled on Hazel also appear in *Battle of Angels* and *Orpheus Descending*. In the autobiographical play, *Something Cloudy, Something Clear*, Hazel appears as herself to speak to the Williams character about their shared past. And I had read in numerous sources that the character of La Niña in *Red Devil* was based on Hazel.

Chris brought me a copy of *The Red Devil Battery Sign* from McKeldin Library where he works, and I began reading it immediately. What I found was especially intriguing, for it turned out that the character of Terrence McCabe was far more nuanced than I had anticipated, neither fully bad nor fully good.

Red Devil was one of Williams' last plays, and opinions about it vary a great deal. Numerous critics denounced it as a failure, but the play also had its supporters as well. It has a strange and surreal plot and marks a striking departure from early works like *The Glass Menagerie* and *A Streetcar Named Desire*. Its storyline centers on a man named King Del Rey, the former leader of a mariachi band, now living in Dallas and dying of a brain tumor, and a woman referred to only as the Woman Downtown, the abused daughter of a crooked Texas politician. She and King are having an affair. King's beloved daughter, La Niña, unexpectedly returns home with her lover, the man that Williams names Terrence McCabe.

I noted early in my reading that La Niña was a nightclub singer. This certainly resonated with what I knew of Hazel, her singing talent and her performances at the "730" club in Madison. I was especially struck to find that La Niña, along with her father and the band, were booked to play at the famous Hotel Reforma in Mexico City. Williams knew at the time of writing *Red Devil* of Hazel's death in Mexico City in 1951. I wondered if perhaps he knew something of this period in her life that I did not.

I thought again about Williams' knowledge of how Hazel had died when I came to an interesting scene between King and his lover, The Woman Downtown, in her hotel room. She reaches for a drink, and he says to her, "I got a serious request to make of you. Don't drink no more in bed."

When she replies that she resorts to drinking for comfort, that it helps "to obliterate experience," King says, "There's no future in it. No. I take that back, there is a future in it and it's a bitch of a future." I couldn't help feeling that his words were tied somehow to Hazel's sad surrender to alcohol and pills.[25]

In a subsequent scene, his admonition is reiterated when she again reaches for a bottle of liquor:

KING: Put down that bottle.

[She doesn't.]

I don't like what you're doing. There's no future in it.

WOMAN DOWNTOWN: Just to wash down a pill, can't swallow it dry.

KING: You're going to wind up not young anymore, not beautiful, not elegant, but—

WOMAN DOWNTOWN: Yes, yes, puta!

KING: The kind that's picked up by any stranger and banged in alleys and back of trucks...[26]

It seems strange that if Williams intended to base the character of La Niña on Hazel that he would write her as the daughter, rather than the lover, of the main character, King. But Williams implies that sort of relationship by a remark that King's scorned wife, Perla, makes to him when he mentions his memories of singing duets with La Niña: "'*Si, recuerdo*,' she snaps. 'Love songs between father and daughter. Not natural, not right.'"[27]

When La Niña returns home with her married lover, Terrence McCabe, King is crushed at the sight of her, for she seems to him irrevocably changed from the innocent girl he knew: "[La Niña enters the kitchen area, nervously meeting the cold scrutiny of her father. She is still beautiful, but the fresh young being which King remembers has been lost and he regards her as if she had criminally robbed him of it now as he faces death...]"[28]

I couldn't help wondering when I read this particular stage direction if Tom had felt this way upon seeing Hazel later in life. In the years immediately following her marriage, she and Dad had traveled often to St. Louis to see her family, and consequently, Tom as well. But once Tom's career had begun to take off, and his professional activities had taken him out of Missouri, I suspect that those reunions ceased. By the time they saw each other again, Hazel may have changed a great deal from the young girl he remembered.

La Niña introduces her lover to her father, and he does not react well:

LA NIÑA: Papa, this is Terrence McCabe.

[There is another moment of silence. McCabe deposits groceries awkwardly, shuffles forward and extends a shaky hand to King.]

MCCABE: [In a hollow, pleading voice]: Hi, Pop.

KING: —Who the fuck is this man calling me "Pop"?

LA NIÑA:—Daddy, he's a—friend of—[Her voice expires.]

PERLA: He's the man who followed her down here …

LA NIÑA: We stayed outside; we thought you'd prepare him for—

KING: Words—don't prepare—for appearance. Christ, you do look like a tramp.

[McCabe circles La Niña into his arms. A great emotional violence rises in King.][29]

Here McCabe is introduced as the interloper, the threat, the rival, which surely must have been how Tom viewed Dad that long-ago evening in 1935.

King tells McCabe he would like to speak to him out in the yard, away from the women, but his brain tumor has made him so dizzy and weak that he must request McCabe's assistance in doing so. He asks McCabe to make it seem as though they are walking companionably rather than reveal the truth, which is that King is leaning heavily on McCabe for support. Once outside, King is in such pain that he sends McCabe back into the house to get him a Demerol. Upon returning, King is in such bad condition that he even requires assistance in taking the pill. In his weakened state and unheard by the women, King questions McCabe about how he became involved with La Niña:

MCCABE: My life before I met Niña was – vacant as that... vacant...

[He gestures toward the Wasteland.]

KING: -- Dump heap?

MCCABE: Yes, empty, empty. Emptiness filled with violence! Oh, I tried to occupy, to satisfy myself with statistics...

KING: Occupy with stat? Lift up your goddam crybaby head and speak plain to me! Chico!

MCCABE: Statistics on buyer-consumption—response to—promotion—commercials.[30]

This was a detail I found very interesting. So this was the career that Williams gave to his character, Terrence McCabe. A statistician. My father was an economist by training. A marketing specialist. In fact, when he had worked briefly for the United Nations, his job title had been "statistician." Could this be a coincidence? Perhaps. But I didn't think so.

The conversation continues and the two make peace. They come to an understanding and acceptance of one another. Even a wary respect.

*   *   *

On the first day of June 2013, my sister Terri shared with me a story that she had never told me before. While I was away at college, back in the late '70s, my mother confided in her about a promise my father had asked her to make when they got married.

"We've both been married before," he told her. "We both have pasts with other people. But let's put that behind us now and start fresh. I have a trunk where I intend to place all traces of my marriage to Hazel—photographs, letters, keepsakes. I bought a lock for the trunk. I will hang on to all of those memories, but will never speak of them with you. You do the same with all of your photographs and letters from Bob. I want this to be a new beginning for us."

Terri was incredulous that my mother had agreed to this.

"Weren't you curious?" she asked my mother. "Didn't you want to know what he was hiding in that trunk?"

My mother claimed that she had never thought about it, but Terri pressed her, until finally, she conceded that yes, at times, she had wondered what was inside.

"Do you remember that trunk?" Terri asked me. "It was in the back part of the basement, behind the staircase."

The image of a large steamer trunk, dark red with black trim, rose up in my mind from the depths of many decades. Yes! I remembered it. I had passed it many times throughout my childhood and never given it a second thought. The memory of it now was suddenly so vivid that I could see the fine coating of dust across the top of it, could smell the damp scent of the basement air.

"I convinced Mom that we needed to find out what was inside," she said. "It wasn't too hard. I think she really wanted to know. So we went downstairs, dragged it out and broke the lock. It took a long time to do it, too."

"What did you find?"

Terri shrugged. "Honestly, I don't remember much. A lot of photos. Files. Letters. The only thing I remember distinctly was some form we found that was related to their marriage. It indicated they had been divorced."

"What? But Mom always told us that she had died."

"I think that's just what Daddy had told her. I guess he thought she wouldn't approve of his having been divorced."

"Are you sure about this?"

Terri paused. "Yes… I think so. It's been a very long time."

"But what happened to the trunk? Where is it?"

"I don't know."

My mother had been alone for many years after my father died. But in 1986, she married again, to a man who sang with her in the church choir. She sold the house I grew up in, the home where she had lived with my father since 1955. Was it possible that she had thrown away all of the things in that trunk? And what had become of all of my father's files, neatly catalogued in the gray filing cabinets in his office? Were those gone, too? It seemed to me impossible, but then, I am a saver, a hoarder, a collector of all of the many words, markers and talismans of my past. I can scarcely bear to throw away anything. My mother was not saddled with this affliction.

Somehow I had managed to end up with some of my father's things: Hazel's photo album, a family scrapbook, most of his plays, the two full-length books he had written, and various odds and ends that bore witness to his life. But there were gaping holes in this collection of artifacts. So much was missing—and what was missing contained all of the answers I now wanted.

*   *   *

The versions of my father that Tennessee Williams created in his plays was not the man that I, or my family knew. But then, we didn't know everything.

Certainly my mother never fully knew my father. She knew the man whose big laugh filled the house, the man who teased her and tried to kiss her while she was cooking dinner, who came through the front door each evening with a lollipop in each overcoat pocket for his girls. But she did not know this man who had locked twenty years away in a steamer trunk and shoved it under the basement stairs.

When she and Terri had opened that trunk, had gone through all of the secrets sheathed in yellowing envelopes, the files that attested to truths she had never known, I can't imagine how my mother must have felt. Perhaps it was like losing my father a second time. But then, is it possible to lose a person that one has never really known?

There has been more than one man in my own life who has kept secrets from me – secrets that, when revealed, destroyed the relationships. Perhaps it was not the secrets themselves that broke my heart and moved me to end things. Perhaps it was really the loss of trust that made whatever love I had felt disintegrate.

What made these transgressions even harder to bear was that I had to keep them to myself. Each time one of my marriages failed, I felt ashamed and concerned that others saw me as a failure, as well. A self-righteous voice in me longed to cry out, "But wait—you don't know the whole story!" I wanted others to know how hard I had tried to salvage those unions. The trouble was, those stories were not mine alone to tell. Other lives could be damaged if I made public what had occurred. Even though I had been hurt myself, what good would come out of revealing dark details to others? I wonder, sometimes, if my father's silence about Hazel had less to do with his own shame and more to do with a desire not to desecrate her memory.

How much honesty did my father owe to my mother? How much honesty did he owe to Terri and me, his daughters? I suppose there are legitimate reasons to keep certain kinds of information from one's children, but it seems to me that a husband and wife owe each other something more. Complete honesty.

More than ever, I needed to find out what information Dad had kept from Mom. I wanted to absolve him, but first I had to understand what the sin was that he had been attempting to hide.

THREE CHILDHOODS

At first I could look at Hazel only through the eyes of Tennessee Williams. What she had been like as a girl was revealed solely by the impression she had left on Tom when he was a very young man, and that view was narrow and most likely misleading. But I was nonetheless thankful that there was any view at all. I read every book either by or about Williams that I could get my hands on, and slowly, an image of Hazel took shape in my mind. An image emerged for me of young Tom, as well. And while their lives were intertwining in those years that followed World War I, my father was growing up in very humble circumstances in the icy landscape of Superior, Wisconsin, wholly unaware that the woman he would one day marry and the man whose heart he would one day break were living just 559 miles south of him.

Tennessee Williams spent the majority of his years before the age of seven in Clarksdale, Mississippi, a "rough river port" that prospered in the years immediately following World War I. This town, which Williams saw as an exemplary model of the Old South, providing him the happiest years of his childhood, would later be refigured in many of his stories and plays. As an adult, he remarked that, "the South once had a way of life I am just old enough to remember—a culture that had grace, elegance… an inbred culture… not a society based on money, as in the North. I write out of regret for that."[31]

As an English teacher, I have often taught *A Streetcar Named Desire* and have seen firsthand how Blanche Dubois represents a romanticized world that is dying, a gracious and aristocratic Old South that is crumbling away, unable to withstand the fast-paced and industrialized society that emerged after WWII, a brash and impatient world of which Stanley Kowalski is the emblem and flag bearer.

In Clarksdale, Tom lived with his mother Edwina, his sister Rose, and his maternal grandparents, with whom he was very close. His father traveled often for his job, and consequently, the family saw Cornelius Williams infrequently, which proved a blessing for Tom, who never got along with him. Cornelius' marriage to Tom's mother was not a happy one, and was given to frequent arguments, so that the long periods of time when Cornelius was on the road gave Tom and Rose the only peaceful family life they ever knew. But all of that would change when Cornelius was transferred to St. Louis to work onsite at The International Shoe Company, a company where Hazel's grandfather, Emil Kramer, worked in a managerial position.

Perhaps what drew Tom and Hazel together was how strikingly similar Hazel's family situation was to Tom's. Both spent their earliest years with absent fathers, clinging mothers, and grandparents who were an everyday part of their lives. When Hazel's mother, Florence, and her father, Franklin Madison White, divorced when she was just a year old, Florence moved back home with the baby to live with her parents. Hazel was only two when Frank formally relinquished his rights as her father and allowed her to be legally adopted by her grandparents. At this time, he was absolved of paying any kind of alimony or child support, and in exchange, he agreed to cease any attempts to contact her.[32]

When I finally tracked down newspaper accounts of Florence and Frank's bitter divorce, reported in the *St. Louis Post-Dispatch*

in June 1913, the scandalous nature of the proceedings startled me. The lively and angry scenes and accusations of their
breakup were splashed all over the front pages for all of their
neighbors to see. St. Louis readers sat down with their morning
coffee and learned how Florence had obtained a divorce from
Frank, as well as custody of seven-month-old Hazel, claiming
that her husband was "as cold as ice." She went on to declare "he
had no affection in his makeup and that he left the house every
morning without kissing her." When the judge asked her if she
had been aware of her husband's habits before she married him,
Florence replied, "A girl does many foolish things and overlooks
faults when she is in love. Anyhow, when a young man is court-
ing a woman he is always on his best behavior."[33]

Apparently, Frank's good behavior did not last long, if one
believes Florence's side of the story. She charged that Frank
"drank to excess, abused her and broke furniture in their home."
On one particular evening she contended that "he struck her
repeatedly on the arms and hands with an umbrella." On another
occasion, she alleged that Frank "broke the chandelier in her
bedroom, smashed a rocking chair into splinters, and threw a
suitcase at her."[34]

Florence told the court that she had hoped the birth of the
baby would bring about a change in Frank's treatment of her, but
she was disappointed and left with Hazel to return to her parents'
home. According to the court records of the divorce proceedings,
Florence testified that on an evening shortly after this, Frank
"arrived at her father and mother's house just before dinner" and
came into her room "with a strong odor of liquor on his breath,
and began to curse." She went on to say that at the dinner table
and in the presence of her father, mother and sister, he "arose
from the table, smashed a chair on the floor, assuming a threaten-
ing attitude" toward her and told her "he had stood all of her he
wanted, and said 'God Damn your soul to hell,'" and then turned
to her father and mother and cursed and abused them.[35]

The worst of it for Hazel was that her mother claimed that her father showed no interest in her. He made excuses not to visit his wife and child in the hospital after Hazel's birth, and Florence told the court that though her husband seemed very fond of other children, he showed no love or affection for their own child.[36] Was this true, or was it the exaggerated charge of an angry and spurned woman?

Frank denied her claims. The *Dispatch* reports that "White said he did everything he could for her comfort and contended his actions had been misjudged and wrongly interpreted by her. He also was affectionate with the baby, he said." The baby's nurse also testified that Frank was loving and kind with his daughter.[37]

Testimony was also given by Frank's law partner who reported that Florence had apparently harassed Frank at the law office by calling over 300 times.[38] Was this an exaggeration, or had Florence exhibited some melodramatic behavior herself? It is impossible to know for sure, but I would eventually read my own father's stories about Florence, and he depicted her as a woman given to hysteria and highly manipulative behavior.[39]

What is clear is that Hazel was born into a very volatile and unhappy home, and although her circumstances were much quieter and calmer once she moved in with her grandparents, they may still have been far less than ideal.

The home Hazel grew up in on Forest Park Boulevard in St. Louis was both grand and dreary. Lyle Leverich refers to it as "a large, dark house,"[40] and later I would discover that my own father described the house as having an "unyielding rigidity."[41] I wonder if part of the reason it seemed like a gloomy and unwelcoming place was because of the personalities of her grandparents.

Leverich describes them as a "small couple who paid little or no attention to any of their granddaughter's friends."[42] They were indeed tiny. In one of the photos I have from Hazel's album, my father, who was 6'0", towers over them both as the three stand together on the Kramers' back lawn. Neither of them seemed to have been accustomed to smiling. Emma Kramer would occasionally muster a slight upturn of the mouth that at least was not a frown, but Emil appears stern and humorless in every photograph I have seen of him.

Emil, or EJ as the family called him, held a managerial position at the International Shoe Company, where Tom's father was now working. Although Tom's mother maintained that Cornelius had a higher status in the company, the fact was that the Kramers' social standing in St. Louis was superior to that of the Williams family.[43] And while Tom's family spent its early years in a series of cramped apartments, the Kramer house was large and spacious, and they regularly employed a full-time maid. Emil made an astonishing amount of money in the stock market, and both he and Emma were obsessively fixated on their wealth.[44]

Though they were not warm and emotionally demonstrative people, they nonetheless provided their granddaughter with every material advantage. When it came time to send Hazel to school, they paid to send her to the prestigious Mary Institute, a private academy for girls, while Tom attended several of the public schools. She was always impeccably dressed in the latest fashions, and at one point, Emma had her bedroom completely done over with all new furniture as a surprise for her. If EJ did not show his granddaughter his love with outward affection, he seems to have tried to compensate for it by buying her valuable stocks and bonds. I can only imagine that this demonstration of love through money left its mark on her character and what she valued.[45]

Hazel's mother, Florence, is often described in various books on Williams as being exuberant, loud and fun-loving, but more likely she was an unhappy woman who masked her frustrations beneath a show of madcap gaiety, and when Tom came to know her, he found her fascinating and lively. In Williams' own words from his book *Memoirs*, "Miss Florence covered up her desperation at home by a great animation and gusto of manner when she was out."[46] Leverich writes that "Miss Florence declared that she would rather be a divorcee than an old maid, but it was an outward manner, thinly disguising her disappointment in love. She had been hastily courted and as summarily dropped after her marriage to a socially prominent ne'er-do-well."[47]

Whatever Florence's feelings had been about the breakup of her marriage to Frank, and about the subjugation she had to endure upon her return to the home of her demanding parents, her feelings for her daughter were deep, intense, and even obsessive. The possessive style of mothering that she practiced, pointedly observed by Hazel's good friend, Esmeralda,[48] would later be underscored for me when I found my father's own depiction of his overbearing mother-in-law.

In this way, she was not unlike Tom's mother, Edwina. Bitterly unhappy in her marriage to Cornelius, she channeled all of her emotional and loving nature into her children. Edwina's intensity, social vivacity and somewhat melodramatic conversational style would become important facets of the character of Amanda Wingfield in *The Glass Menagerie*.

At first, when the Williamses moved to St. Louis, Tom was captivated by the crowds and excitement of a town far larger than sleepy little Clarksdale. But he would come to loathe St. Louis. According to Williams' scholar, Allean Hale, Tom would later refer to his new home as "that dreaded city," the city of St. Pollution. Hale wrote an essay entitled "Tennessee Williams's St. Louis Blues," and it is worth quoting here what she had to say about the initial culture shock Tom experienced in this new environment:

Tom, sensing his mother's misery at the move, would always see St. Louis through her eyes. As the Episcopal rector's daughter in a town of 6,000, Edwina had enjoyed social prestige. Now, in the fifth largest city of the United States, she was nobody. With a reverse snobbery, she impressed on her children that St. Louis was a town where only status mattered. They could not hope to attend private schools: Mary Institute, where a girl was enrolled at birth, or the Country Day School, where the Bishop's grandson who was Tom's age attended. Years later Williams would still remember: "That name, public school, kept stabbing at my guts till I wanted, as old as I was, to sit down and cry." He wrote that in St. Louis he first learned that there were the rich and the poor and that they were poor. The sense of being an outsider would become a dominant theme in his writing.[49]

While Hazel and Tom were drawing nearer to the time when they would meet, my father was growing up in Superior, Wisconsin, the firstborn child of William and Magdalene McCabe, in far poorer circumstances than Hazel or Tom would ever know.

My father wrote extensively about Superior and his growing-up years in his manuscript entitled *A Superior View*. Of this bitterly cold, far-North settlement where he grew up, Dad wrote that it was "a gusty town at the head of Lake Superior. The town [...] belied its name; it was a rough, tough town, the terminus of five major railroads and the winter hangout of such sundry characters as railroad boomers and would-be woodsmen and the summer home of legitimate woodsmen attempting to live a three- or four-month's life of ease on their hard-earned money."

He would later add, "Superior was a hard-drinking town. Not only did it have some very accomplished indigenous imbibers, but it was host to lumberjacks, sailors and miners whose work kept them from the fleshpots of civilization for long periods and who, once on the town and with earnings in their pockets, would acknowledge few peers among the established and settled citizenry."[50]

This was hardly the genteel, refined and romantic South in which Tom grew up, or the thriving city with its rigid social hierarchy where Hazel was born. It was a place that was friendly only to those who learned early how to negotiate it.

Like Hazel and Tom, Dad had also been raised in large part by his grandparents, Cyrus and Ida McCabe, who came to live with the family when his younger brother, Robert, was born; they never moved away. Dad was luckier than both Hazel and Tom, though, when it came to his parents and family harmony. Of his mother and father, he wrote that besides being "poor but honest," they "were completely in love with each other," and as a result of that stable and happy relationship, my father "skimmed the cream." He maintains that he "went everywhere, was let in on everything, was treated as a grown-up" from the time he could remember. Regarding his father, Will McCabe, Dad wrote that, "he seldom went anywhere without taking me along."[51]

While Tom's father and Hazel's grandfather were involved in business and worked at white-collar jobs, my grandfather's background was decidedly blue-collar, though he would eventually become involved to a small degree in local politics. Dad writes:

> By occupation my father was an engineman – which meant that he was first a locomotive fireman and later a locomotive engineer [...] From the beginning of his employment, Dad was a stanch union man in Local 257 [...] He was rewarded with local offices and finally elected Chairman of the Wisconsin Legislative Board of the Brotherhood and became the Wisconsin representative of the National Board. One of his most prized accomplishments was being one of the railway labor representatives who worked with President Truman to avert a major railroad strike in 1946.[52]

Dad's family lived in a rented house that lacked a basement, "a prime requisite" in places as cold as Superior. "To conserve heat in the winter, the foundation would be covered with tar paper, perhaps to two or three thicknesses. At the first snow, which usually stayed the winter, we banked the snow against the tar paper, building up a very efficient insulating wall."[53]

Eventually Will bought the house, but it was a modest bungalow that bore no resemblance to the imposing estate where Dad's future wife was growing up. The difference in their backgrounds, both social and economic, would one day cause friction between my father and Hazel's family.

In four mammoth volumes, *A Superior View* is an imposing read, and Dad never did find a publisher for it, though he tried relentlessly throughout my childhood. On the day of my father's funeral, his best friend, Ernie, approached me and said, "Now it is your job to try to find a publisher for your Dad's book."

This was a fairly staggering assignment to give a 16-year-old girl, buckled with grief and the many insecurities that beset me throughout my adolescence. But I never forgot his words. Those four volumes have been stored, packed and restored over the years, with no thought to taking on Ernie's proposed mission. But as I have begun investigating Dad and Hazel over this last year, I finally began turning the pages of *A Superior View*, and what I have discovered has been a real gift. I don't think the book would ever have found a publisher; it is too long, too specific to a very narrow section of America, and is bogged down under the weight of what even Dad called his "expansive proclivities," but it has yielded to me numerous stories about my father's childhood and the town where he grew up. Perhaps quoting just a bit of it in these pages will do more than simply add counterbalance to the stories of Hazel's and Tom's youths. Perhaps it will allow me to imagine that I have done my duty to my father and brought to light at least some of the words he worked on for so many years.

*   *   *

Tom Williams met Hazel one spring day in 1922. At the time, he was eleven and Hazel was nine. Williams recounts the meeting in his *Memoirs:*

> One afternoon I heard a child screaming in the back alley of the street. Some young hoods were, for some unknown reason, throwing rocks at a plump little girl. I went to her defense; we took flight into her house and all the way up to the attic. Thus began my closest childhood friendship which ripened into a romantic attachment [...]
>
> We started spending every afternoon in her attic. Being imaginative children, we invented many games, but the chief diversion that I recall was illustrating stories that we made up. Hazel drew better than I and I made up better stories."[54]

I would eventually encounter a vivid description of this attic when I stumbled upon my father's account of his marriage to Hazel. On his first trip to St. Louis to meet her family, he quickly learned where he would rank in the Kramer household, and how dimly her mother and grandparents looked upon her union with this poor railroad man's son; he discovered that the room to which he had been assigned was a musty attic room across a hall from the maid's room. No doubt this was the same room in which Tom and Hazel had played:

> The only window was a small, dirty one about shoulder height between the wide, inverted 'V' where the roof sloped down [...] A partially enameled chair was partially hidden by the open door. A small, twenty-five watt bulb dangled from a long cord; it was the only light in the room. A white enameled cot stood with its head against the east wall. The white spread had a square patch exactly in the center. A cardboard clothes closet stood flanking the bed. On

the other side of the window, along the wall, was another enameled monstrosity, a battered white commode. The inevitable enamel washbasin and pitcher were sitting on its marble top. [...] There were no towels.[55]

This "bedroom" was only the first of the indignities to which he would be subjected by the Kramers for daring to fall in love with their pampered Hazel.

While Tom and Hazel were forming their decades-long friendship, far away in Wisconsin, my father had just become a teenager. While Tom was defending the bullies that accosted Hazel, my father was involved in some fights of his own. Will McCabe had converted a high-ceilinged woodshed adjoining their house into a small gymnasium for his son, in order that he might learn the manly arts and be equipped to defend himself against the town ruffians, of which it appears there were many. Dad's father was "bound that I was going to be able to defend myself, in spite of the extreme pacifist leanings of my grandfather [...] A punching bag and pulley weights were put up along the wall. A trapeze was installed and some mats laid down."

But Cyrus, who was Dad's primary male caretaker while Will was away on railroad duty, allowed Dad "no opportunities to determine my burgeoning pugilistic ability. As soon as a dispute started it was ended by his peremptorily ordering me in the house, taking full use of the opportunity to inveigh against physical violence as a means of settling disputes."

One day, Dad and the three Mosely boys next door got into an argument and faced with the numbers aligned against him, as well as Mrs. Mosely wielding her formidable hairbrush, Dad took off for home but was stopped in his tracks by Will, who had watched the whole episode unfold:

"Get back there," he told me, "and get what you want."
I protested. "They'll hit me."

"Of course," he said, "and you'll hit them back."

"But she's got a brush," I said, nodding in Mrs. Mosely's direction.

"Never mind the brush; I'll handle that," he attempted to assure me.

I was still not convinced. "There are three of them," I pointed out plaintively.

"Then get over with your back by the fence so they can't get behind you," was his advice. Then he added a warning. "And if you don't lick all three of them, I will give you a licking."

The ensuing fight turned out to be anticlimactic when the Mosely boys' mother deserted them, leaving them without the added defense of her hairbrush. A few punches were thrown, and then Will called an end to it. Later, Will and Cyrus got into a hot debate of their own over the lesson Will was teaching my father about physical violence. Dad concludes this story with the remark, "It was shortly after this that the gymnasium was dismantled."[56]

*　　　*　　　*

The same year that Tom met Hazel, his mother gave him a gift that went a long way toward setting him on the path he would take to become a writer. Edwina writes:

> At an early age Tom started to write and seemed to be writing much of the time. Writing was his talent. When he was eleven, I decided to buy him a typewriter, thinking it would make the writing easier [...] It was large and clumsy and sounded like a thrashing machine but Tom was delighted with it. I could hear him hitting the keys for hours.[57]

Edwina revered reading and books, and she had instilled this love in Tom and his sister, Rose. Cornelius once complained to a friend "that when he got home from work, he usually found his wife in the living room reading a book, Rose in her room reading a book, Tom out on the fire escape reading a book."[58]

In her book, *Remember Me To Tom,* Edwina reveals that "Cornelius looked on Tom's writing as effeminate and a waste of time. His tirades were often directed against it. When the electric bill rose a dollar, he blamed this crime on Tom. 'You're just spoiling him,' he accused me. 'He sits writing all night and runs up the light bill.'"[59]

My father also loved to read, and unlike the dismissive attitude Cornelius conveyed to his son, Will McCabe had a great deal to do with my father's lifelong love of books. He read voraciously and widely, always taking the maximum number of four books during each visit to the library. He always took my father along and made sure he had some books of his own. In writing about the house he grew up in, Dad said:

> A luxuriant grape vine covered the south half of our porch. There were never any grapes, but the foliage made a spot, sheltered from most summer weather, which I put to good use by hitching up a porch swing. It would hold two persons, but when I felt lazy or a ball game was rained out, I occupied it in various positions, but always in pleasurable company. Tom Sawyer, Huck Finn, Hans Brinker were among the many who shared it with me.[60]

As far as I know, Dad didn't spend any of his youth writing stories or poems. He was an avid athlete, and generally used whatever free time he had involved in a neighborhood game or practicing his batting. But something changed as he grew older. By the time he and Hazel were married, Dad began writing. I have kept and treasure all that he left behind him: short stories, a novel, memoirs, the book about Superior, and at least a dozen plays.

I believe that it was Tom who inspired my father to attempt writing drama. After he and Hazel married, there were quite a lot of occasions when the three of them would socialize. As Tom began to have success in the mid-1930s having plays produced, my father certainly would have noted this. Was he envious of Tom's gift and success? Did he feel competitive with him, given that they both had fallen in love with the same woman? Or did Tom encourage my father, perhaps even reading some of his early scripts and offering critiques?

I may never know for sure, but two memories from my childhood lead me to believe that some sort of friendship did exist between Dad and Tennessee Williams, at least during the first few years after Dad married Hazel. When my sister and I were young, every Christmas we both would receive the gift of a children's book from a friend of my father's who lived in New York, a woman named Audrey Wood. I distinctly remember writing thank-you notes each December 26th to Miss Wood, though I had no idea that this woman was the agent of the famous Tennessee Williams. Did Williams put my father in touch with Miss Wood? It seems to me very likely that this was what happened.

The second memory I have was from a day when I was seventeen, shortly after my father died. I spent a long afternoon in his basement office, going through all of the correspondence he so painstakingly kept carbons of in his gray filing cabinets. I found a number of letters Dad had written to Elia Kazan, the famous director with whom Williams had had a close working relationship. How had Dad gotten Kazan's address? The letters seemed to imply that Kazan had written back. How else would my father have known this man, if not for some assistance from Tom Williams?

*   *   *

By the mid- to late-1920s, Tom and Hazel's relationship had progressed from a childhood friendship to a romantic relationship. Writing about Hazel at this point in time, Williams remarks that "she had extraordinary beautiful legs and her breasts developed early; she was inclined to plumpness, like her mother (who was sort of a butterball) but she had a good deal of height. In fact, when I was sixteen and Hazel fourteen, she had already outdistanced me in stature and had begun her habit of crouching over a little when she walked alongside me in public lest I be embarrassed by the disparity in our heights."[61]

It was at about this time that Tom developed a problem with blushing, turning red when anyone's eyes, male or female, met with his. This new affliction even manifested itself in his relationship with Hazel, though he had known her now for five years. Williams remembers that this new habit greatly surprised both Hazel and her mother, and moved Hazel to remark to Tom one day on a crowded streetcar, "Tom, don't you know I'd never say anything to hurt you?"

Williams goes on to say, "This was, indeed, the truth: Hazel never, never said a word to hurt me during the eleven years of our close companionship, which, on my part, ripened into that full emotional dependence which is popularly known as love."[62]

I can't help but note that Williams qualifies Hazel's sparing of his feelings to the first eleven years of their friendship. This would mean that after 1933, things may have changed. Certainly, upon hearing that she had fallen in love with my father, and whatever Hazel may have said privately to Tom about this new relationship, Tom may have found that Hazel's words hurt a good deal more than they once had.

Williams writes very openly about the early sexual feelings that Hazel awakened in him. Perhaps the most explicit of all his memories occurred when they were alone together on the deck of a river steamer:

She wore a pale green chiffon party dress with no sleeves and we went up on the dark upper deck and I put my arm about those delicious shoulders and I 'came' in my white flannels.

How embarrassed I was! No mention was made between us of the telltale wet spot on my pants front but Hazel said, "Let's stay up here and walk around the deck, I don't think we ought to dance now."[63]

At about the same time that Tom was having his first sexual feelings and experiences, my father was also finding himself thinking about females in ways he never had during his childhood years. A regular hangout for Dad and his male friends was the local "Y", which had a pool where only males were permitted to swim. However, pressure was being exerted to allow the facility to be opened to women:

This, our first evidence that the clamor of women for equal rights meant dislodging the males from entrenched positions, was not to be taken lying down [...]

Came the first night of the young ladies' revels and we found that someone had cut a small, but utilitarian hole, in one of the colored glass windows of the pool area. Whoever had taken the time and effort to make it had put it in a spot which was unlikely to be noticed.

There was considerable bickering as to who was to view in what order, but the pushing quickly evaporated when the first viewer announced, despondently, "They're wearing suits."

And so they were. Instead of swimming in the buff as we did, the girls wore long, skirted bathing suits...

I don't know whether the hole was ever used again. If it were, the positions of the sexes were reversed.[64]

Dad also mentions that he had a few casual dates with a girl named Marian, "which included nothing more intense than a movie or a sit-in evening, much of which was spent in conversation with loquacious parents." In his junior year, a friend of Dad's telephoned Marian, pretending to be Dad, and asked her to the Junior Prom. The friend thought this would be hilarious because Dad did not know how to dance. When Marian later called Dad to ask him what time he'd be picking her up, he silently scrambled to figure out what was going on. Knowing full well that someone had played a trick on him, he nonetheless dressed in his best suit, borrowed the car and took Marian to the prom.

Later, he shared the story with his parents. Dad's birthday was shortly after this, and in private, away from his father, my grandmother gave Dad a gift of dancing lessons at a studio in Duluth. She also paid the tuition for any girl he might like to take along and told him to keep the lessons a secret from Will:

> My father never learned to dance and wasn't going to make himself ridiculous by trying it now. So at parties, Dad sat on the sidelines while Mom danced with other women. She was a good dancer and it was not unusual for one of the other men to claim her for a dance while Dad pretended not to notice.
>
> Somehow, Dad found out about the lessons and started to call me "The Dancer." It was more an epithet than a nickname.
>
> Mother felt she was more than repaid when I would dance with her.[65]

*   *   *

After Tom graduated from high school, he prepared to attend the University of Missouri, and he expected that the following year, after Hazel would graduate from The Mary Institute, that she would join him. But Tom's father Cornelius did not want Tom's St. Louis girlfriend attending the same school as his son. He had never approved of Hazel, looking down on her flashy, divorced mother, and believed that her presence at the University of Missouri would prove a distraction and keep Tom from doing well in school.

According to Edwina, Cornelius told Hazel's grandfather that Tom would not be allowed to attend the university if Hazel did. Edwina believed that Cornelius held more power in the company than Emil Kramer did and assumed that Emil might have been concerned that his job was in jeopardy. However, Hazel's good friend Esme believed that it was actually Emil Kramer who sought to keep the two apart. Whether the decision was made by only one of the men or whether they concurred on the matter, the result was the same. When the time came, Hazel was enrolled at The University of Wisconsin instead of at Missouri.[66]

Perhaps neither of them needed to have worried, for while in her senior year of high school, with Tom off at college, Hazel had begun going steady with another boy, Ed Meisenbach.[67] Later, she would tell my father of her relationship with Tom that he was her best friend, "but that's because we grew up together. I couldn't ever think of Tom as but a friend."[68]

Once Dad and Hazel were married, they returned often to St. Louis so that she could visit her family. It is clear from her letters and from a letter Tom wrote in January of 1938, as well as from passages in my father's book *The Distant Hill,* that a friendship existed between the three of them for some time.

Dad and Hazel had been in St. Louis for Christmas of 1937, and in January of 1938, Tom wrote to his grandparents from a hotel in La Salle, Illinois, on his way back to the school he was attending at that time, the University of Iowa: "I drove up here with Hazel and Terry on their way to Madison."[69] Did the three of them stay in that La Salle hotel that night? It seems likely.

Whatever the exact truth was about Tom and Hazel's relationship while they were in their teens, it is clear that they were very
close, and that Tom felt that he was in love with her. Who knows
what would have happened to the two of them had Hazel been
permitted to attend the University of Missouri. By the time he
attended college, Williams was already experiencing some feelings of attraction to other males, and most likely, the two would
have slowly drifted apart.

But perhaps because of the manipulative way that both
Cornelius and Emil contrived to keep the two apart, Tom seemed
to have greatly romanticized Hazel in his memory. He maintains
that she was the greatest love of his life, even more than the men
that followed.

Tom's brother Dakin has suggested that Tom might have had
a chance at a heterosexual life if only he and Hazel had married,
a view entirely at odds with what is now known about sexuality.
Dakin's daughter, Francesca Williams, told me that her father
"turned a blind eye to the truth in spite of the facts" and that
it might simply have been "wishful thinking," as homosexuality went against his and the family's religious beliefs. Francesca
added that "Tom would've been miserable in a heterosexual
marriage," and he would have "eventually come out anyway."[70]

One thing is certain. Had Hazel not been sent to the University
of Wisconsin, she would never have met and fallen in love with
my father. And I most likely never would have been born, for
if my father had married another woman, one with whom he
might have formed a lifelong bond, then he would never have
dated and married my mother. Strangely, it seems I owe my
very existence to the machinations of Cornelius Williams and
Emil Kramer, and to a woman who broke at least two hearts: my
father's and Tom Williams'.

The Distant Hill

After my father died, a month before I turned seventeen, I was stunned at my loss.

He had entered the hospital in September of 1973 for what was to have been routine gall bladder surgery. At least, I had been told that it was routine. So had my mother. If my father had known something more alarming about his condition, he had not shared it with us. Following his surgery, Mom told me that he was "in worse shape than the doctor had thought." This vague statement was never clarified for me, and, strangely, I must not have pushed for a more detailed answer.

I remember those autumn months leading up to his death in early December the way that one remembers a bad dream after waking. Some of it is still vivid to me, and other parts have blurred with time. Instead of coming home fairly soon after his operation, he remained in the hospital with what my mother referred to as "complications." At some point, he also developed pneumonia. September turned into October. Every weekend my mother would ask me to accompany her to the hospital to visit him, and I am ashamed to say that I think I went only one time.

I remember that visit. The stark white walls, the strong antiseptic smell. The heart monitor with its green line that peaked and plummeted. The man in the bed who was my father but did not look like him, who had trouble speaking. After a few moments, I went out and sat down in the hallway, lightheaded and shaky. I was deeply upset and very afraid, but I did not confide this to my mother. I kept it inside, though I am sure she knew.

In November, after Dad had rallied to a degree and was feeling better, he insisted that he wanted to go home. He told the doctor that he was sure he would get better if he could just be back in his own house with his family. The doctor strongly advised against it, but my father insisted. I was both excited and frightened by his return that day. He was very white, very thin, and had to be carried into the house and up the stairs to my parents' room. I wanted to speak to him, but my mother shooed me and my sister away.

"Later," she said. "He needs to rest."

But later never came. In the middle of the night his condition took a downward turn, and he began to spit up blood. My mother called for an ambulance. My father left the house on a stretcher, my mother following. Terri and I huddled together on the couch, frightened and quiet. It was the last time that we saw him alive.

Several weeks later, on December 3rd, he suffered a cardiac arrest. Apparently, he had buzzed numerous times for the call nurse, but she had been late in responding, and he was no longer breathing by the time she arrived. He did not survive.

My life had been a perfect and safe bubble up until that time. Suddenly, Daddy was gone. I had been wholly his girl up until my early teen years, when I began to go through all of the painful fits and starts of adolescence, of breaking away from the tight hold of one's parents. My father had tried to hang onto the close relationship we had always enjoyed, but at thirteen, I began to strain against that hold. He was hurt, I know, when I turned down his invitations to accompany him to the hardware store on a Saturday morning, or to join him in the street after dinner for a game of kickball. Had I known how soon I would lose him, my budding quest for independence would never have flowered. But I didn't know.

And after he died, I was consumed with a guilt and regret unlike anything I had ever experienced in my short life. I would have given anything to have him back again and tortured myself with recriminations, with memories of all the ways I had so recently failed him as a daughter. At the time, I had an after-school job at the public library shelving books. In those months immediately following Dad's death, I remember more than a few times wheeling my cart back into the foreign language section, which few people seemed to visit, sitting down on one of the low stools there, and sobbing.

I think this was when I first attempted to talk to the dead. I have always wanted to believe in ghosts. I like the idea that I will continue somewhere, and not simply cease to be, and that I will be reunited with all of my family members who had gone on before me. So instead of praying to God, whom I felt had forsaken me, I would instead "pray" to my father, talk to him as though he were still there and could hear me. I remember one night I wrote him a letter and laid it out on the table next to my bed, the pen placed carefully beside it. I begged him to come to me that night, to pick up the pen and answer me. In the morning, I shot out of bed to look at the letter for his reply. And, of course, there was nothing there. And after a time, whatever hope I had died out. Time filled in the hurt, and I stopped trying to resurrect my father.

At least, I did until a minor character in a late-career Tennessee Williams play introduced me to a man I'd never known, and the woman he had once loved. My quest to learn more about this unknown aspect of my father and the life he had lived before I was born sent me back to the plays and books he had written and that I had hung onto over many years.

Of course I had read my father's writing before. Each time I went through the stored boxes, I turned the pages and let my eyes travel over the words there. But the truth is, when I had read his work previously, it had been before I had learned much about Dad's first marriage or about Hazel's sad life and death. Perhaps if I were to look at it again, something would jump out at me that I had never noticed before.

And this is precisely what happened.

I picked up Dad's early novel, *The Distant Hill.* I had never paid too much attention to it before and truthfully, had never read beyond the first page. The opening introduced a character named Lizbeth who was a sorority girl in what was clearly the 1930s. She is looking out a window, musing about the weather, and frankly, it didn't interest me at all.[71] I remember I had always thought this an odd storyline for Dad to have been pursuing. But suddenly, I began to notice things that I had never thought to look for before.

The main character's name was Lizbeth Kemmerer. Hazel's middle name was Elizabeth, and her last name, Kramer, was very close to Kemmerer. I read on, and my certainty grew. Lizbeth was a singer, just as Hazel was. She was from St. Louis, had attended an all-girls school there, and called her mother "Mush." The main male character was named Mike Shane, an Irish name, and he was an instructor of economics, just as my Dad had been. The story was set in Madison at the University of Wisconsin. As Mike becomes involved with Lizbeth, he nicknames her "Red," because of her chestnut red hair.[72]

As I read deeper into the book, the similarities between the story and real life continued to accumulate. Lizbeth had grown up in the home of her grandparents, who had adopted her after her parents divorced. And Lizbeth's mother's name wasn't disguised at all; she was named Florence. Florence is a difficult person who takes an instant dislike to "Mike," and resents his relationship with Lizbeth. At home in St. Louis, Lizbeth has a good friend named Tom Burton, who writes plays which are being produced locally, and is clearly modeled after a young

Tennessee Williams. And Mike's father is a railroad engineer, just as my grandfather actually was.

It seemed that with every new chapter of the 521-page book, some additional detail would further convince me that *The Distant Hill* was less a novel, as my father labeled it, than a very thinly-veiled memoir of his marriage to Hazel. Although I could not look upon each revelation as an indisputable statement of fact, I felt sure that what I was reading was extremely close to what had really occurred. So many of the details and developments within the story were corroborated by information I already knew and was learning all the time. Reading the book felt to me as though my father had pulled up a chair beside me and said, "Mel, I see you've been trying to research my first marriage. So here, let me clue you in on a few things you don't know."

*   *   *

The novel tells the story of Lizbeth Kemmerer, a sorority girl at the University of Wisconsin during the 1930s who meets and falls in love with a graduate student named Mike Shane.

Though Lizbeth and Mike have other dates before a prom near the beginning of the story, while at the prom they dance together and discuss Lizbeth's most recent singing engagement at the local Campus Club, which Mike attended. Mike tells her:

> "I'd like to hear you again. Maybe you can sing my favorite, 'Star Dust.'"
> "It's a favorite of mine, too."
> "Then it's a promise?"

Later, Mike muses about her and it is clear he is smitten. He remembers, "those enormous brown eyes that seemed utterly unable to hide the thoughts behind them; the charm of her tumbled chestnut hair."

By this time, I had looked at innumerable photographs of Hazel. It wouldn't be until later that I saw a color photograph of her with her red hair, but I had read a great deal about it. I had, however, seen ample evidence of those large brown eyes that seemed so wide and expressive. It felt strange reading my father's praises for a female other than my mother.

I don't remember my parents' marriage lacking in affection, but to my eyes, it certainly did not seem to be a romantic one. Dad would make playful overtures to my mother as she stood at the stove, and she'd laugh and give him a little shove. "Go on with you now," she'd say. "I have to get dinner on the table."

One year, a day before their anniversary, my sister and I were horrified when Dad pulled us aside to show us the fancy new vacuum cleaner he had bought for Mom as a gift. I believe I was about thirteen at the time, and was especially scornful that he did not realize that this was not the sort of present a man gave his wife to commemorate their love.

"That's awful," I told him. "That's not romantic at all."

He looked crestfallen, but I didn't realize how seriously he had taken our dismay until the next night at dinner when he handed my mother a small box wrapped in shiny paper and topped with a bow. She opened it to find a beautiful pearl choker.

Dad looked over at me and raised his eyebrows meaningfully. I nodded and laughed.

I think he gave her the vacuum cleaner, too, but that part is hazier in my memory. My father was a very loving man, but I do not remember him as a man swept away by wild emotions or given to extravagant gestures. If there was any great passion between my parents, it was not something that Terri and I ever saw.

And so this glimpse into my father's past, this view of him as a starry-eyed young man falling in love, was a revelation to me.

*   *   *

Of course, young love has its adversaries. Dad's description of Mike meeting Florence, Lizbeth's mother, leaves little doubt of Mike's feelings about the character and Dad's about his actual mother-in-law:

> Their laughter was interrupted by a clackety-clack on the stairs as a short, roly-poly woman came bouncing down like a punctured rubber ball. The fingers on her left hand, which held the metal handrail, bore a plethora of rings, over which the flesh curled and rolled. She wore, as so many dumpy women seemed to do, a low-cut white dress, which made her look even more roly-poly than she was. [...] She had spent a lot of time and energy on her make-up; he couldn't help wondering just what she would look like with all that powder, rouge and mascara washed off.
>
> She was so completely the antithesis of Lizbeth, who was tall and lithe. It was hard to believe that they were mother and daughter.

As Mike and Lizbeth grow closer, Lizbeth explains to Mike about her unusual circumstances growing up after he makes the mistaken assumption that Florence must be living with her former husband's parents, since her name was the same as theirs. Not a bit of this speech is any different than the one that Hazel must have long ago made to my father: "Mother was divorced shortly after I was born, and Grandmother and Grandfather adopted me and gave me their name. Mother got her maiden name back, but kept the 'Mrs.' because, after all, I was her daughter."

What is apparent from this passage is how embarrassed by the situation Lizbeth is. The reader senses that she was questioned on this topic many times, and she has grown used to having to explain it. I believe that Hazel, too, must also have felt this way about her circumstances, and must have longed for a more traditional story, and a father who had stayed in her life.

At one point in the novel, Lizbeth and Florence get into an argument about Lizbeth's developing relationship with Mike. Florence is threatened by this relationship because she sees Mike as a rival for Lizbeth's affection and fears he will supplant her. After the argument, Florence ruminates on what was said and about her past:

> Mrs. Kemmerer's thoughts tumbled backwards. Would it have been different, as Lizbeth had said, had she not had her mother and father to help meet the problem of Jim Stayner's irresponsibility? She thought not. In fact she knew they couldn't have gone along from crisis to crisis, Jim jauntily, airily, without an apparent care in the world while she carried the burden for them both.
>
> As she remembered it now she had spent no time in useless grievance over what should have been. She was no longer a wife but she was a mother and she had dedicated her life to being the best; nothing was allowed to interfere with her duties to Lizbeth, the only thing Jim had given her. She made it clear to her friends that her baby had first claim on her, and all of them, without exception, had remarked on the fact that she was such a wonderful mother. She had given everything to Lizbeth and asked nothing. She had worried over her childhood illnesses, tucked her into bed and crept in with her until she was asleep, and was there each morning to give herself afresh when Lizbeth opened her eyes. Never, since theirs had been a love above everything else, did she ever entertain the thought that Lizbeth might ever find a love, a loyalty, outside herself.

A number of things in this passage seemed uncannily similar to me to things I had read in Lyle Leverich's book, *Tom*. In referring to Florence Kramer's husband, Frank White, Leverich refers to him as "a socially prominent ne'er-do-well" and indicates that

Florence had been "hastily courted and as summarily dropped" after Hazel's grandparents had made it known to him "that they were not about to support their daughter's husband in the fashion to which he was accustomed." It appears that this information was shared with Leverich by Esmeralda Mayes, Hazel's best friend while they were growing up.

Mayes had gone on to share what she had witnessed of Florence's possessive nature in her role as Hazel's mother: "Miss Florence drew Hazel's bath and put the toothpaste on her toothbrush—and in the morning the milk and sugar were already on her cereal—and Miss Florence would say, 'That's the least I can do for Hazel!'"

This portrait of an intensely over-involved mother is echoed in Dad's book, when, while visiting the Kramers, he enters the bathroom hoping to shave and finds the following scene:

A large electric heater was hooked up and its Cyclopean eye gave off a bright red glow that filled the room with enervating heat. Steaming water filled the tub; a soaped face cloth lay over the soap dish. The water basin was filled with fresh, hot water. Cosmetic jars and powder were on its marble top. A toothbrush, complete with paste spread on its bristles, stood next to a tumbler of mouthwash.

Mike turned off the heater. He whistled a tune as he took off his shirt and hung it on the closed door. He turned to get his shaving kit on the card table when the door flew open and Mrs. Kemmerer stood there.

"Hi, Mush. Do you always break in…?"

"What are you doing?"

Mike rubbed his chin. "Well, I thought I'd shave and then run some cold water in the tub; it would cook a lobster that way."

"You can't." Mrs. Kemmerer's face got red and she plugged in the heater again. "I ran that for Lizbeth."

"Oh, and here I thought you had done it for me," he laughed, and put his hand on her shoulder.

She drew away with a frown. "Now what," she said, "would give you that idea? This is for Lizbeth."

I have stared often at the photograph I have of Hazel's home on Forest Park Boulevard, especially at the third floor where it would seem that my father had slept, banished there by Florence instead of offered one of the more comfortable and pleasant rooms on the second floor. I am sure my father was acutely aware of their coldness to him, and knowing Dad, I am equally certain that he would have done everything in his power to win them over. How unfamiliar the stiff, remote Kramers must have seemed to him, coming as he did from a close-knit Irish family, whose open affection for one another was never diminished, even in the midst of frequent and vocal "branigans," as Dad called the lively family disagreements.

On the front steps of the house, which is photographed from a distance adequate to include the entire imposing structure, stand a tiny girl and an adult woman close beside her. The figures are too small to say with assurance who they are, but I think it very likely that they must be Hazel and her mother. The effect of the miniature figures against the backdrop of the mammoth house is such that they appear to be enveloped by it. Is it what I know of her family that makes the house seem cold, almost malevolent, or is there truly something sad about the two pictured here, dwarfed by the house that holds them?

Many of the earlier chapters in *The Distant Hill* take place in St. Louis, as Lizbeth is frequently called home to visit her mother and to attend to the various emotional calamities that seem to befall her. In chapter 11, Dad introduces the character of Tom Burton, who is indisputably modeled after a young Tom Williams. Although he is mentioned very early in the book as a former beau of Lizbeth's—whom she says she could never think of as anything but a friend—in this chapter he and Lizbeth inter-act alone and for some time.

Tom shows up at the front door just as Lizbeth is gathering clothes to take to the dry cleaners. She is preparing to leave St. Louis to return to Madison and school. Tom stays to dinner at the Kemmerer house that night, and in his conversation with Florence, it is quite apparent that nothing has been changed here but the last name:

> Never had Lizbeth seen her mother more animated, more talkative at a meal. Only once did she give Tom a chance to say anything [...] She asked him how his folks were and listened carefully to his statement that his father was well and was wondering when Mr. Kemmerer was going back to work, nodded sympathetically over his recita-tion of his mother's delicate health. It might have been Esther's arrival with the main course of cold cuts and potato salad, but he didn't finish telling about Rosalind and David.

Two things are dramatically clear to me in reading this pas-sage. It is more than that the character is obviously intended to be Williams. This can be seen plainly by the father figure who works with Lizbeth's grandfather at the International Shoe Company, by the mother who is seen as something of an invalid, and by the siblings Dad includes for Tom Burton; he names them Rosalind and David, while Tennessee Williams' siblings names were Rose and Dakin. What is remarkably clear to me is how well my father seems to have known the details of Tom's family life. I know that Hazel and my father spent time with Tom on numerous occasions when they visited St. Louis, but I can't be absolutely sure of how well they knew each other. This passage, and other details in the book, seem to point to their having known each other very well indeed.

Later, when Tom and Lizbeth are alone, Tom, who is then training as a bookkeeper or accountant, confides in her his dreams for his future:

"I never want to see a double entry ledger or a cost sheet again. Never!" he said intensely.

With the wisdom of intuition Lizbeth didn't interrupt. "Remember," he continued, "how I liked to write and how I sold a few of my stories to 'Weird Stories' and 'Ghost Tales?'" Lizbeth nodded, remembering how he had brought over his first check, for ten dollars, to show her and how they had pretended to shiver when the story appeared. "That's what I should be doing. Writing. And that is what I am going to do."

He looked at her with a mute appeal for approval. "I am glad, Tom," was all she could think of to say. "I am glad your father has finally seen it your way."

Tom jumped to his feet. "He doesn't know it yet…"

Lizbeth sat up straight in her chair, her hands clenched. She could feel the tears of sympathetic anger welling in her eyes. "Damn!" she cried dismally, "damn! Why can't people be happy?"

"The privilege of parenthood, the privilege to cast, to mold, either with or without understanding." He laughed mirthlessly. "Well, I have some money from this summer and I have some saved so I won't be dependent on the privilege necessarily."

Tom goes on to tell Lizbeth that he will be returning to college, and that nothing will stand in his way. This is, of course, precisely the path of Williams' life.

Later in the book, Tom runs into Lizbeth when she is home for another visit because her grandfather has had a stroke. This is also straight-out of Hazel's real life, as her grandfather, E.J., did have a stroke. When Tom and Lizbeth run into each other at a restaurant, he fills her in on the work he is doing: "The Mummers are putting on my latest one act play, that's why I am in town." The two of them end up going together to one of the rehearsals.

What does the continual appearance and reappearance of Tom in Dad's book indicate? Certainly that he was a very close friend of Hazel's, and that my father was aware of the importance he had for her. But something more, I think. Even then my father was an aspiring writer. At the time he met Tom Williams, his efforts seem to have been primarily channeled into the writing of short stories. But after he came to know Tom, there was a shift in his focus. This marks the period when Dad began to write plays. I have no doubt he was influenced by his acquaintance with Williams, and as time went on, by witnessing the successes that came Tom's way.

My father had always craved success as a writer. It is heart-breaking to me now, as I comb through all of the creative work that my father produced during those years, to be made aware of just how avidly, relentlessly, he sought this success. I believe that Williams was for my father both an inspiration and a thorn in his side. He sought to emulate Tom's path, in hopes that he, too, could experience the heady exhilaration of having his work produced. In fact, I have even found some of Dad's work that bears a pen name he had chosen for himself: Terry Williams. I will grant that William was actually my father's middle name, but his choice of using it as his last name seems transparent to me and makes me feel a sadness and tenderness for Dad that now has nowhere to go but inside of me, as it is too late to share it with him.

*   *   *

Late in the book, the strain on Mike's and Lizbeth's marriage grows more serious and unrelenting. Mike is temporarily suspended from his job in Madison because he is being investigated for taking Lizbeth with him on business trips. I wondered whether or not there was any truth to this plot point. There was nothing about any such investigation in my father's employment file, but perhaps because the investigation ultimately proved that there was nothing inappropriate occurring, the whole incident may have been expunged from his record.

Unfortunately for Mike and Lizbeth, this unsettling development occurs while Florence is visiting them in Madison. Efforts are made to hide the truth from her, but she eventually finds out. She confronts Mike and accuses him of making Lizbeth miserable:

> "I understand what it's doing to Lizbeth," Mrs. Kemmerer said. She stood up. "She's going to pieces; she's drinking too much lately. But you probably didn't notice that, soaring on your lofty sentiments."
>
> "You really don't like me, do you? You dislike me so much—not because of what I am but because of Lizbeth – that you are blind. I know Lizbeth has been drinking and as you, yourself, said very pertinently, lately. Lately, do you understand. It's you, not I, who are responsible for that, you and your actions."
>
> Mrs. Kemmerer's mouth dropped open, then she shut it, her lips in a pinched, thin line. She turned and walked out of the room.

Apparently, Florence is so incensed by this exchange that she becomes ill, and a doctor is consulted. It is clear throughout the story that many of Florence's illnesses are either brought on by her emotions or feigned in hopes of achieving some end.

There is also the issue of Lizbeth's substance abuse. In the scene in which Lizbeth informs Mike of this latest development in Florence's health, there is ample evidence of her drinking problem:

As Mike turned the car into Lake Court he saw Lizbeth get up from the porch step and run down the street toward him. There was a swaying, stumbling urgency about the way she ran that filled him with dread. He had left that morning, early, before anyone else was up, and since then something had happened. He braked the car to a stop and jumped out. He noticed Lizbeth's disheveled appearance, her blood-shot, red-rimmed eyes before she lurched into his arms and buried her head in his shoulder.

"Honey, Honey, what is it? What's wrong?"

His only answer were her broken sobs. He held her close until they stopped, then he walked her to the car. He sat her on the seat and wiped her eyes.

"Did you think I had left you?" He tried to laugh.

"Oh, Mike, what happened last night? What happened?"

"Nothing happened."

"But something did with you and Mother. Now she's sick."

"Sick? Pull your legs into the car and we'll go home."

Lizbeth shook her head violently. "I don't want to go home. I want to talk to you. Here in the car." She slurred her words.

That the character Lizbeth has a drinking problem ties in all too neatly with what I have learned of Hazel. But there's something new in *The Distant Hill*: Dad seems to attribute the beginnings of her alcoholism with the guilt inflicted on her by her mother, and later, the guilt she inflicted on herself after Florence died. It's hard to know if this is accurate, or just my father blaming everything that went wrong on the mother-in-law who caused him so much grief.

Near the end of the book, Mike has taken another job in Des Moines, Iowa, and they are living there happily until all goes awry in the late winter of 1943. It had appeared that things were improving for Florence. She was living alone in St. Louis in the family home, which had been deeded over to her, and she had found a job. Her involvement in something outside of her obsessive mothering has resulted in her distancing herself a bit from the young couple, and it seems briefly as though things might work out for Mike and Lizbeth after all. Lizbeth remarks that everything is "perfect, almost too good to be true:" "The remark was prophetic, although at first they didn't recognize it. The first inkling was through Mrs. Kemmerer's letters. She complained that working and keeping the big house were too much for her, even with Esther's help."

While Lizbeth is trying to decide what to do to help her mother, the decision was taken out of their hands. A neighbor, Mr. Lane, wrote her. Lizbeth read his letter to Mike:

Dear Mrs. Shane: I was going to have Mrs. Lane write you, but I finally decided to write you myself. I think that you should know that your mother isn't well. She has either lost or given up her job and does nothing but sit home all day. Lately she has suffered such moods of depression that she has Esther scared to death. Esther told me last night that she was actually thinking of leaving, which, in itself, is quite serious since Esther has been with your family for some time.

She won't have a doctor. She has absolutely forbidden Esther to call Dr. Lee and Esther is too frightened to go against her orders. I hesitate to do so because your mother will blame Esther for telling me. I am sure you are the only person who can have any influence with your mother.

The letter sends Lizbeth immediately to St. Louis.

When I first read this section back in the summer of 2013, I had no idea of what illness might have befallen Florence. I rather assumed it might be more of her staged sicknesses, feigned to elicit a reaction from Lizbeth. I would later learn the truth: Florence had been diagnosed with cancer, and the prognosis was grim.

Hazel had taken her mother on a trip to California after leaving for St. Louis. Efforts were made to keep Florence from knowing just how sick she was, and it was hoped that the warm climate would help her. But she grew sicker and eventually, returned with Hazel to live out the remainder of her days in Des Moines.

To surmise what those last days were like, I have only to look at the final chapter of *The Distant Hill*. It would appear that it was a hellish experience for all three of them, one that brought my father—or at least his stand-in—to a mental state so dark he seemed almost unrecognizable. When an acquaintance at work asks him where he is going, he answers, "Home," and this sets off a chain of unspoken thoughts: "Home. To open the door and be sucked into the maelstrom of recrimination. To hold out a hand of help in the eddying pool, to feel the touch of willing fingers, grasping, holding your hand. Then nothing. Gone. A bobbing head in tears."

The acquaintance, trying to coerce Mike into going out for a drink, urges him, "Forget your wife for awhile."

"Forget your wife, like forgetting to breathe. Forget her when she was in his mind's arms every waking minute. Forget her when he couldn't forget her even in his dreams, those horrible extensions of his waking fears."

Then the acquaintance continues, "Come over to my house and I'll give you a drink—all you want. Pep you up."

To this, Mike thinks, "Ha! I'll show you how it can dull, a dull numbing, a mental anesthetic, a stumbling walking through the day. A retreat from thinking, from feeling, a liquid hand upon the mind. Come over to my house and I'll show you these things, all these things."

Lizbeth drinks to cope with the incessant demands placed on her by her invalid mother, and Mike joins her to blot out the bleak misery that their lives have become. Later, as Mike enters his house, he finds Lizbeth drunk, coping with her mother's insistent and critical demands. Clearly this has been what their days and nights have been like since Florence came to stay with them.

When Florence dies it is after a period where she has been crying and calling out to her daughter. Lizbeth does not go to her, but rather, stays in the kitchen and drinks. When she finally goes to her and sees her mother's lifeless body, this discovery topples Lizbeth over the edge of the despair she has already been walking along, and she falls apart completely—hysterical, sobbing, and full of self-recriminations. Though Mike tries to comfort her, to help her, to love her, she pushes him away. Mike comes home one evening shortly after Florence's death to find Lizbeth's suitcases in the living room: "They had cleaved apart, been cleaved apart by this thing that had come between them; she stood on one side in sorrow, agony, desolation, and he on the other in desire, longing, his reasoning voice unlistened to, unheard."

Lizbeth tells him she can no longer stay there in the house in Des Moines, but when Mike offers to leave with her, to find another place, she tells him she does not want him along. She tells him that this is the way her mother would have wanted it. She cries out, "'I never should have married.'"

When he learns of Lizbeth's intentions to leave, Mike is devastated:

He sank into a chair. So this was the answer she had reached, searched for so long and come up with this. The pattern all over again. Licked, beaten, defeated by it at every turn and now again. Retreat to this. And there was nothing he could do, nothing. He could not force himself upon her, coerce her to his will. If this is what she wanted, this she must have, she should have it.

The train takes her away to Wisconsin, and this is the end of the book. But Dad leaves Mike and the reader some hope. Mike urges Lizbeth to see their friend Robbie when she gets there. Robbie is a professor who had been a mature and nurturing presence to both of them. It is plain to see that Mike hopes Robbie will convince her to return to her husband, even though Mike's pleas have done nothing to sway her.

The last two sentences of the book are, "From deep within him hope stirred again. The stars still shone."

And it would seem that the hope was not misguided. Dad left Des Moines behind, got a job and an apartment in New York, and Hazel had joined him. And it seemed as though all had worked out. At least, for a time.

I can feel a great deal of empathy for both Hazel and my father. I know what it is for a marriage not to go swiftly and cleanly to its end, but instead, to falter, limp forward, and then backslide, not once, but sometimes multiple times, before both parties give it up as unrevivable. It had certainly happened to me. Each time a small hope would be rekindled that all was not lost, that whatever was wrong could be fixed. And then that flame would go out yet again.

*   *   *

When I was still a teenager, the woman my mother told me about all those many years ago, my father's red-haired bride, took on the hazy outline of a villain. A femme fatale who captivated and toyed with men and then cast them aside. A shady woman with dark secrets who must have deserved what happened to her. It was true that she had broken Tennessee Williams' heart, and that she then went on to break my father's. I had no doubt of that then. And I have no doubt of it now.

What surprises me, now that I have pieced through so much of her life, is how much I have come to care about her.

How difficult must it have been for her to grow up knowing that her father gave her away? To have to own up to friends that her parents were divorced in 1913, when she was just a baby, at a time when divorce was almost unheard of, certainly among "respectable" women? To have to cope with a mother who was possessive, demanding, and immature? Who tried to compensate for the loss of her husband by placing an unnaturally heavy emphasis on her relationship with her daughter?

My father's work, though it was born of his heartbreak after the dissolution of his marriage, has done far more for me than simply revealing facts about his life with Hazel. It has brought me closer to both of them, to the sorrow and disappointment that they felt when their lives took turns they hadn't planned on. In the past, I had sometimes thought that my father would have been disappointed in me if he had lived to see my marriages fail. But now, for the first time I began to consider another possibility. That maybe he would have drawn me aside and put his arm around my shoulder. Maybe he would have leaned in close to whisper, "It's okay, Mel. I've been there, too."

Hazel Asks For Help

In the spring of 1947, Hazel was in desperate need of help. She was already living apart from my father, and her grandfather and mother had died one right after the other, in 1942 and 1943. Then in April of 1947, Hazel's grandmother, Emma, joined them. In what must have felt to Hazel like both a terrible blow and a devastating betrayal, she learned that the inheritance that she had expected to come to her from her grandmother's will was not coming to her after all.

In just five years, she had lost almost all of her closest family members, as well as the emotional support of her husband of more than a decade. At this difficult and sad time, she reached out to the one person in her past who had always loved her, who had never let her down. She contacted Tom Williams.

They were no longer in close touch with each other and hadn't been since Hazel's mother had gotten sick and left St. Louis. Certainly their lives had spun off in different directions. She had moved from Madison to Milwaukee to Akron to Des Moines in order to follow my father in his career. They had finally ended up in Manhattan. Meanwhile Tom had gone from a struggling and largely unknown playwright to a great success with his break-through play, *The Glass Menagerie*. His life was full of travel and writing and excess of all sorts, and she must have wondered at least a little if his star had shot so high that he would no longer have the time or inclination to help her. It is clear that she didn't even have a personal address at which to reach him, for she sent her message to him via his agent, Audrey Wood.

When I first spoke to John Bak about the character of Terrence McCabe, we'd written back and forth about other topics related to Tom and Hazel. One thing he told me that interested me very much was that there was a letter from Hazel to Williams at The Harry Ransom Center in Austin, Texas, which he had not yet seen. At the time, this had surprised me. Bak is a noted Tennessee Williams scholar and has done extensive research into Williams' life. If he hadn't seen it, maybe none of the other scholars had either. There might yet be some new information for me to discover.

A quick Google search of the Harry Ransom Center's Tennessee Williams Archive revealed the letter from Hazel to Tom. I contacted a man named Rick Watson, the head of reference for the Williams holdings at the Center. After some minor bureaucratic paperwork, Rick sent me Hazel's letter, and this letter sent my quest off in an entirely new direction. It was dated May 18, 1947.

Dear Tom:

I am contesting my Grandmother's will inasmuch as I was cut off with only a nominal bequest.

My attorney, Mr. William W. Crowdus of 506 Olive Street, St. Louis, Mo., was in New York this last week-end and tried to get in touch with you but you were out of the city.

The background of my case is important; that is, how my grandparents treated me and how I treated them when I lived at home after they adopted me. Would you please write to Mr. Crowdus and tell him everything you remember as to how my Grandmother treated me and how I acted towards her?[73]

Hazel went on to ask Tom many specific questions about his memories about her relationship with her grandmother. Later in the letter, she brought up her aunt:

> If you ever met my Aunt, Mrs. Hazel Bagby, please narrate anything you may have heard her say—either about my Mother, Florence, or me; or any remarks she may have made regarding my grandparents' estate or financial matters. Further, if you ever saw my Aunt and me together I would like you to tell how I treated her.

Near the end of the letter, she added, "I should have explained that in my contest of my Grandmother's will, I am contending that she was unduly influenced by Mrs. Bagby, who, under the will, receives by far the lion's share."

She included both her home and work telephone numbers so that he might call her and signed the letter, "My best to you as always, Hazel McCabe."[74]

This letter was really the first time I had ever heard her "voice," and I was able to get a sense of how she expressed herself. Even more important than that, the subject of the letter opened wide a whole new avenue of research to me—one that I would explore to great advantage.

Years before I began this research into Dad's first marriage, I had stumbled onto something online about this very court case. Knowing the name of my father's first wife, on a whim one day I had done a search of her name and come up with a site that provided a three-page synopsis of Hazel's challenge of her grandmother's will. It had been clear to me upon reading it that it involved Hazel and members of her family, but I recall that at the time, I had found it very hard to follow. The fact that her aunt, whom she challenges in this case, was also named Hazel made reading the document confusing. Moreover, at the time, I didn't know anything about her adoption, her grandparents, or her father, Frank. Hazel was still a stranger to me then.

Now I returned to that site. I knew so much more about her life than I had when I first encountered it, and all of it suddenly seemed perfectly clear. Hazel felt her aunt had poisoned her grandmother's mind against her and succeeded in getting her grandmother to change her will very shortly before she died. This "last-minute" will provided Hazel with only a nominal bequest from the estate and left what amounted to a great deal of money to her aunt.

Looking at it this second time, I now saw things that I had missed or not understood the first time. Information was provided about Hazel's father Frank and how she had come to be adopted by the Kramers. And surprisingly, I suddenly noticed that my own grandmother was listed as one of the witnesses who had testified for Hazel's side.[75]

And another thing became clear to me, as well, after I had read Hazel's letter from the Ransom Center.

"You know that Tom must have complied with her request," I said to Chris. "He was crazy about her."

Chris agreed. "He would certainly have tried to help her."

"That means," I continued, "that somewhere, there is a letter from Tennessee Williams to Hazel's lawyer, discussing in great detail his memories of life in Hazel's home when they knew each other as children. A letter that I'll bet no one else even suspects exists."

"That would be quite a find," Chris said.

"It would for sure."

I decided that I would do everything in my power to find it.

*   *   *

I did not know exactly what Hazel would have been doing after she left my father. Money was not a problem, because of the bequests left to her when her grandfather and mother died, and so finding a job to support herself might not have been absolutely necessary. However, she did have ambitions. She loved music and had sung in clubs and even on the radio while at the University of Wisconsin. It seemed likely to me that she would have continued with this passion, perhaps hoping to make a real name for herself in the arts-rich world of New York City.

I made another search of the listing of Williams' correspondence at the Harry Ransom Center and turned up a name that I had missed before: William W. Crowdus, Hazel's lawyer. Excited that this must be Tom's letter, written in response to Hazel's plea, I put in a request for it.

While I waited for the letter to be sent, I followed up on something that had caught my eye as soon as I had read Hazel's message to Tom. She had given him two telephone numbers. Obviously, her home number would now be assigned to someone else, but what about the work number? I googled the number and found that it belonged to the Belvedere Hotel in Manhattan, a small hotel right in the heart of the theater district.

I went immediately to Ancestry and looked in its file of old City Directories. From previous searching, I already knew Hazel was listed in the 1947 Manhattan directory, at her apartment on W. 71st Street. This time, I looked up the Belvedere Hotel. Yes, there it was, with the exact same phone number that it was assigned in 2013.

Hazel had added "Extension 149" after the phone number. What did that extension indicate? A specific department within the hotel? A room number? If she had worked at the Belvedere, what had been her job? She could have perhaps been a secretary. Or maybe she was involved in entertainment in some way. Perhaps she had found a way to continue her singing.

I wrote an email to Michael Link, the manager of the Belvedere, to find out what he could tell me. Unfortunately, it was not much. When I ask about the extension she had given, he said, "All of our current extensions are 4 digits. Ext. 149 could mean anything. Sorry, I know I haven't been much help, but that was over 60 years ago and much has changed with the hotel since then."[76]

So it seemed that this was a dead end. I abandoned it for the time being but kept it in the back of my mind. Maybe I could figure out a way to learn more.

Meanwhile, I received the letter from the Ransom Center that I was waiting for, and it, too, turned out to be a disappointment.

Instead of being a letter *from* Williams *to* Crowdus, it turned out to be the reverse. What the letter did prove, however, was that Tom had indeed written the letter that Hazel requested.

The letter was dated June 3, 1947.

Dear Mr. Williams:

Thank you very much for your very interesting letter of May 22, 1947, regarding Hazel McCabe's home life with her grandparents, Mr. and Mrs. E.J. Kramer. I hate to put you to too much trouble, but I would appreciate your answering the following queries, as in a matter of this kind we need specific information.

What followed were sixteen questions for Williams to answer, all related to how Hazel treated her grandparents and her aunt, how they treated her and her mother, and if there had been discussions about Hazel's future inheritance while Tom was present. At only one point did Crowdus quote from the letter that Williams had written: "You mention that Hazel Bagby 'was particularly cold and resentful in her attitude towards Miss Florence.'"[77] Crowdus went on to ask Williams to give him specific facts to prove this.

I felt certain that Tom would have replied to Crowdus' letter, supplying the facts that Hazel needed him to give. And so, somewhere, there must be two letters from Tennessee Williams that I needed to find.

*   *   *

Meanwhile, I continued to try to find someone I could talk to who might have known Hazel. Given that she was born in 1912, my prospects were dim. I would have to concentrate my search on people who were considerably younger than Hazel, who would have known her when they were still children.

I telephoned my cousin Roberta, the daughter of my father's brother, Bob. She is almost twenty years older than me and had been born four years after Dad and Hazel married. She would have been just a young girl through the 1940s when they were together.

Roberta didn't remember much about her, but she did share with me one interesting insight about my grandmother's feelings about her daughter-in-law. She told me that she and Grandpa had liked Hazel well enough but didn't think much of her "wifely" skills. Apparently whenever they would visit the newlyweds, all they would find in the refrigerator were limes and seltzer water. In the words of my Aunt Ann, Roberta's mother, they "ate out all the time and drank too much."[78]

I wondered about this characterization of the life they were leading. How much of it was exaggeration and how much of it was true? I knew from reading *The Distant Hill* that Hazel had made efforts to learn to cook in their early days together, with mixed results. Despite having had no training at all in that area, she tried hard to become what was expected of a good wife during that time period. I can imagine that those societal expectations weighed heavily on her. As someone who also does not cook much and has no talent in this area, I can empathize with her.

I also knew that Dad felt he had fallen into a habit of over-indulgence in alcohol while he was with Hazel, and that he regretted it. Would she have had a problem with alcohol no matter what course her life had taken, or did she fall prey to it out of unhappiness or dissatisfaction with the direction of her life? It was hard not to think about my mother, the woman my father would turn to after this first marriage. My mother rarely drank. Occasionally she would take a few sips of wine, and then complain that it made her dizzy. I can imagine that my father might have welcomed this notable difference between the two Hazels.

Dad had had two very close friends from his days in Wisconsin: a young man named Ed Little, and Marian, who was my father's secretary in Milwaukee. She ended up marrying Ed. I knew Eddie and Marian well when I was growing up, as they were living in Alexandria, Virginia, at the time I was a child. I thought of them as more of an aunt and uncle than simply friends of my father. They lived with Marian's daughter from a previous marriage, Ginger, and Ginger's daughter, Carrie, who was about the same age as I was. I was familiar with Carrie, but her mother, Ginger, was much vaguer in my mind. It seemed whenever we would visit the Littles, Ginger would be out somewhere.

But now it occurred to me that Ginger would have been a teenager during Dad's years with Hazel. She might very well remember Hazel and be able to share some stories with me. But I had no idea how to contact her. I didn't even know her married name.

I googled Eddie's name, knowing I would certainly find something online about him, if not about Marian. Eddie had been the U.S. Ambassador to Chad and would merit some sort of information. It didn't take me long to find an obituary that provided an overview of his career. Through this, I also discovered Ginger and Carrie's last name.

On a whim, I did a Facebook search for Ginger. She would be in her eighties now. Surely a woman of her generation would not be on social media. But there she was. I composed and sent her a message, and waited impatiently for her reply.

Ginger was gracious and talkative, though she didn't know too much more than my cousin Roberta had. She told me that Eddie and Marian had been very surprised when Hazel and Dad had separated, as they had always seemed so happy together. And they had liked Hazel very much. She said that the four of them frequently visited together, and Ginger had a vivid memory of Hazel sitting in their living room, with her "flaming red hair," her big smile and loud laugh. She described her as flamboyant and outgoing.

I asked Ginger if Eddie and Marian had left behind any photographs of Dad and Hazel, or perhaps some letters from my father. She told me that stored in her house she had a "four-foot high pouch of photos and memorabilia."

Four feet high? I was dying to ask her if I could see what was inside.

"I always mean to go through it, but I haven't yet," she told me.[79]

There are times to push, and times to hang back. I didn't see any polite way to ask her if she would let me sit in her basement for half a day and scrounge through that pouch. And so I said nothing.

This has been one of the most difficult things to deal with when approaching people who might be able to help me. My mission is not their mission. They are unlikely to understand my urgency to uncover what might be there. Indeed, there are times when I don't entirely understand it myself.

*   *   *

One of the photographs I had found in Hazel's album that intrigued me more than most was a 5" x 7" shot, placed into a small cardboard frame. The setting of the photo appears to be the interior of an elegant restaurant. Seated at one of the tables, from left to right, are my father, Marian Little, Hazel, and finally, a woman whom I could not identify. The women are all nicely dressed, each wearing a hat. Hazel appears to be wearing a black jacket and a blouse with an ascot of lace. Her matching black hat sits atop her red hair at a jaunty angle. My father is wearing a suit. Everyone in the photo is smiling. It seems to be a happy occasion. Behind the group, there are two waiters in tuxedos. At another table, there is a young and attractive Japanese woman, looking down at her plate of food.

Written across the bottom of the cardboard frame are the words: "Don't think it hasn't been fun. My eleventh post-surgery day and I feel like a million bucks. June 1943, Romayne" (or Romagne—the handwriting did not make it clear). Scrawled in ink across my father's suit and somewhat hard to make out are the words, "The Gang."

The unknown woman did not appear to be anyone in Hazel's family. She certainly wasn't anyone from the McCabe clan. Her hair is light, her skin fair, and she appears to have blue eyes. She looks vaguely Scandinavian. I had found another photo of Hazel and another unknown female sitting astride mules in what looks to be a scene out west. The two mystery women looked like they might possibly be the same person.

I was also perplexed by the word "Romayne" or "Romagne" written at the bottom. The only Romagne I knew was in France. Were they in France for some reason? But it was 1943. The middle of World War II. I googled the word to see if I could find some other town of that name in the United States but had no success.

I was also confused by the remark about "my 11th post-surgery day." I assumed the handwriting on the photo to be Hazel's, presumably meaning that she had just had some kind of surgery. For what? Nothing else I had come across in any of my research had indicated any kind of illness or physical trouble.

But perhaps the most perplexing aspect of all was the juxtaposition of Hazel's dazzling smile and the date, June 1943. If this was indeed the actual date, then it had been less than a month since Hazel's mother, Florence, had died. One of the passages that I had noted and wondered about from Lyle Leverich's book *Tom* was the following:

> Preoccupied with his writing and trying to decide what move to make next, Tom had not seen any of his old St. Louis friends during his stay at home. Hazel, inconsolable in her grief over the recent loss of Miss Florence, had returned to Madison with her husband. In the end, the greater dependency of Hazel upon her mother, even in death, would destroy the lesser bond of her marriage. Tom could only ask himself whether it would have been any different if he and Hazel had married, or whether his would have become the same twisted, embittered married life of Edwina and Cornelius Williams.[80]

Without a doubt, the single best book that I have consulted in my research has been Leverich's. There are footnotes for everything. Rare is it that one finds a paragraph without a textual note. So it makes it all the more surprising—and maddening—that Leverich made this fascinating remark about Hazel's relationship with my father, and yet provided no source.

Where did this information come from? It seems to imply the actual thoughts of Williams. It might have come from a letter from Williams, or from his notebooks, or even something passed on to Leverich from Williams' brother, Dakin.

It is surprising, as well, that there seem to be factual errors in Leverich's assessment. Why would Hazel return to Madison with my father when, at that time, they lived in Des Moines, Iowa? And the statement implies that Hazel had just recently left. The time period referenced here is the winter of 1944, and yet Florence Kramer had died in May of 1943. Had Hazel come home to St. Louis for an extended stay?

If so, it makes the photograph in the restaurant that much harder to understand. Here Hazel is smiling broadly. She does not look at all "inconsolable." If she was grieving the loss of her mother, why is she pictured here in such a festive mood? Why does she say she feels like a million bucks?

The years that followed this photo would be devastating ones for both Hazel and my father. In four years more, they would no longer be married, and four years beyond that, Hazel would be dead.

Down In Mexico

America is a land that keeps track of its dead. If you know where a person died, it usually only takes a little bit of searching through Ancestry or an inquiry to the right government agency to turn up a death certificate that will offer some sort of explanation of what caused the death. It was just this minimal sort of sleuthing that turned up, for example, the death certificate for Emil Kramer, Hazel's grandfather.

Chris found it and emailed a copy to me one morning. "Take a look at how he died," he said.

Emil had died in March of 1942. He had already suffered a stroke, which debilitated him, though I did not learn this information until later in the summer. An avid cigar smoker, he had lit up one late afternoon, fallen asleep with the lit cigar in his hand, and set himself on fire. He died of the burns he received that day.[81]

What a horrible way to go. Who wouldn't feel a measure of pity for anyone who suffered such a death? Apparently, the answer to this question was Tom Williams. He seems to have had no pity at all for the old man. In his book *Lost Friendships*, Donald Windham, a close friend of Williams, reports that he was quite taken aback when Tom, having stumbled upon a news account of Emil's death, burst into wild, nearly maniacal laughter. So intense was his bitterness over the part that Emil had played in separating him and Hazel that Tom felt only a bizarre sort of glee at hearing of the man's tragic end.[82]

Chris and I searched hard for some news account or a death certificate that would solve the mystery of Hazel's last day. Though we knew she had died in Mexico, it seemed nearly impossible to query authorities there. All the same, I did try. I telephoned the American Embassy in Mexico to make inquiries. My call was met with what seemed to me a kind of dumbfounded disbelief. The tone of the woman I spoke with was both amused and astonished; how could anyone be foolish enough to think that death records for someone who had died in 1951 might simply be pulled from a file drawer?

I knew from one of the clippings that Dad had kept that Hazel had been interred at Oak Grove Mausoleum in St. Louis. I decided I would call them. Perhaps they had kept a copy of the death certificate for each person buried there. The man I spoke with on the phone seemed startled by my call. He looked up Hazel's name for me. Yes, he said, she was interred there, but he had no other information. I would need to speak with the woman who managed the mausoleum. I would have to call back the next day.

That night I googled Oak Grove in St. Louis and discovered numerous newspaper reports about the neglected state of its upkeep, the deterioration that had befallen the place in recent years. One link led me to a fascinatingly weird YouTube video, in which a reporter chased and hounded with questions the "owner" of Oak Grove as she walked to her car. She wore her hair in a tall black beehive style and looked quite angry. This, apparently, was the woman I would be speaking with the next day.

On the phone with me in the morning, she was cordial but succinct. No, they did not keep death certificates on file. No, she could not tell me the name of the person who had had Hazel interred there, because there was no name of any individual on file. Her ashes had simply been shipped to them. This was all she knew. I asked if it would be permissible to visit her crypt. Yes, she said, that would be fine.[83]

My younger daughter, Taryn, lived in St. Louis at the time. She told me that before she left, she would drive out to Oak Grove and take photographs of Hazel's last resting place. So, at least I would have some photos, but I still needed to track down the death certificate.

*   *   *

I recently looked at a photograph of Mexico City taken from the air. The view was unlike anything I had ever seen. Building after building after building was jammed into the frame, and the cityscape continued across the hilly terrain for what seemed like hundreds of miles. Even in 1951, when Hazel had been there, *el distrito federal* had been a teeming, noisy, smoggy swirl of humanity. And in spite of her experience living among the thronging hubbub that was New York, there seemed to me to be a vast difference between living as a woman on her own in Manhattan and venturing as a woman alone into a foreign country, knowing no one, perhaps not speaking any Spanish. Was it really possible that she had come here alone, a stranger? I found it difficult to believe. Had there been someone—a man, perhaps even Sam Bern, the last person to see her alive—who had convinced Hazel to follow him into this world so different from the one she had known?

Perhaps she had set her sights on Mexico because of Tom. Beginning in 1940, Mexico was a favorite destination for Williams, and he often traveled here to spend time writing. And he was not alone. In the '40s and '50s, Mexico City was a hotspot for celebrities, writers, musicians and artists. Had Hazel been lured here by the celebrated nightlife, hoping to make some place for herself, and her voice, in one of the many nightclubs?

Certainly anyone who might be able to provide me with any information had died long ago.

*   *   *

In reading Lyle Leverich's book *Tom*, it became clear that one of Tom's and Hazel's closest friends was the young girl named Esmeralda Mayes, whom Leverich interviewed and quoted quite a number of times in his book.

A little sleuthing turned up an obituary online: she had passed away in 2009. One important piece of information that I noted from the obituary was that Esmeralda had two children. A search of her son's name revealed that he, too, had died, but I quickly found her daughter, Esme, living in Pasadena. She was on Facebook.

On June 29th, I wrote her a lengthy message, trying hard not to alarm her by seeming like some sort of lunatic. It must be very disconcerting to be suddenly approached that way by a stranger who is seeking personal information. Along with my message, I included the formal portrait I had of my father and Hazel. A week went by before I heard back from her:

Melanie,

I'm out of the country at the moment but I'll call you when I return next week. My mother would have been 100 this year. She died in 2009 at the age of 96...

I think you are correct about Hazel Kramer and Tom (Tennessee Williams). My memories of what my mother said are hazy at best. My brother Joe who died the same year as my mother was more attentive to these stories. I have his materials. I will endeavor to look through it this summer, but we are traveling quite a bit and it's somewhat buried. We probably should talk as you might awaken some brain cells...

Keep bugging me this summer and I'll try to call you between activities later this month.

Esme Gibson[84]

In Esme it seemed that I had finally found someone willing and able to help me. I settled in to wait for word from her when she returned from her travels.

*   *   *

Unable to locate Hazel's death certificate at either Oak Grove Mausoleum or within the state of Missouri, I was at a loss where to look next. Someone suggested to me that I try the National Archives. It seemed unlikely to me, but what did I have to lose? Nothing, it seemed, for this time I hit pay dirt. I made a formal request for the death certificate and received it by mail. I ripped open the envelope, confident that I was about to discover for sure how she died.

But I was wrong.

The cause of death was filled in, in Spanish, as "congestion visceral generalizada" or general visceral congestion.[85] This sounded incredibly vague to me. I contacted a friend who is a doctor to ask him what he thought. He wrote back:

Without an autopsy, it's usually impossible to know for sure the cause of a seemingly natural death. If it was a suicide, I don't know whether there was an attempt to cover it up and make it seem like a natural death. Visceral congestion just means one or more organs being inundated with fluid. I think this would be the end point of any number of natural or unnatural deaths, but lung congestion would be seen in a death by asphyxiation. Lung congestion would be the only organ that could be so diagnosed absent an autopsy, so maybe that's what the doctor meant. But most likely, the term he used was just his 'garbage pail' term for any death where the cause of death wasn't evident.[86]

I thought it very likely that an effort had been made to cover up a suicide. My cousin had been given an account of her death that I now knew to be false. Robert Bray, the editor of *The Tennessee Williams Review,* had said that this was what he had heard about her death. It may well be that someone had made an effort to cover up a suicide because of the scandal such a death would create.

One surprise the death certificate held was the name of her next-of-kin, the person who had been sent a telegram of her passing. I had expected that it would be my father, but it was not. It was Hazel's own father, Frank M. White. This was really startling information. As far as I had known, he had disappeared from her life when she was an infant. How did the authorities in Mexico know to contact him?

It was indicated on the certificate that there was no known former address for her in the United States. This seemed to indicate that she was not simply in Mexico on vacation. If she were, she presumably would have carried in her purse some form of identification that bore her Manhattan address.

I was spending most of my waking hours ruminating on the information I had uncovered, coming up with even more questions. It had been a long school year, and the search for Dad and Hazel's past now consumed nearly all of my free time. Chris and I decided to take a vacation, though it didn't exactly prove to be a break from the project. I only succeeded in moving it about three hours east, alongside the shore of the Atlantic Ocean.

Rehoboth Beach, Delaware is a place I love dearly and crave through every dreary winter. It is a place that my father had first taken me, back when I was just fifteen years old. Now, with so many thoughts of my father filling my head again, the memory of those Rehoboth trips came back to me with a vividness that was startling. Suddenly, I was remembering not only what had occurred all those years ago, but also, what those events revealed about how much my father had wanted to protect me from the pain of a broken heart.

*   *   *

As we walked into the hotel lobby that first year, I immediately noted the breathtakingly handsome young man with startling blue eyes and a dark tan who tended the front desk. Much to my amazement and joy, he also noted me, and so began the first summer romance I had ever had.

I sensed Paul was older than the boys I knew, and sensed also that if he learned that I was only fifteen, his interest in me would fizzle immediately. And so I lied to him. When asked, I told him that I was seventeen, and this answer did not seem to alarm him. Every evening after his shift at the desk, he would return to the hotel and sit with me beside the green, floodlit waters of the swimming pool, or we would walk along the beach at night, when it was emptied of all its sunbathers and sand-flinging children. And at the end of the evening, we would linger in the cinder-blocked stairwells of the hotel, kissing and clinging and whispering.

My poor father was beside himself. Here it was his vacation. He should be relaxing and having a marvelous time playing on the beach with his daughters. But one of his daughters had transformed overnight into someone he did not know, and he was no doubt deeply suspicious of the intentions of this young man who had come along and taken her from him.

As I crept into the hotel room each night, I could tell that my father was not sleeping. He lay in bed on full alert, unable to drift off until I appeared. I would wash my face, brush my teeth, then slide into the second double bed beside my sister, and only then would the rustling and vigilance from the other bed finally silence.

On the last evening in Rehoboth, feeling guilty for the lie I had told him, I at last confessed my true age to Paul. I hoped against hope that he would laugh, shrug it off, kiss me and tell me that it made no difference. But it didn't happen that way. Instead, he seemed alarmed to learn the truth. He told me he was twenty-one years old, going on twenty-two that November, and that he could not continue our fledgling romance. Perhaps if I was sixteen. But no, not fifteen. Impossible. I was simply too young.

I wept. And implored. All to no avail. That last night, in the cinder-block stairwell, he gave me a swift kiss on the cheek. The sort of kiss reserved for little girls. He told me he would write to me and that we could remain friends. I fled to my hotel room and cried in the bed there until I finally fell asleep. And though my father was deaf, and could not possibly have heard the sounds of my sobbing, I am sure he knew.

Paul did write to me, all through that next year. I waited on his letters, daydreamed over them, and made far more of them, I am sure, than he ever intended. When it came time to plan the next summer's vacation, I begged my father to return to Rehoboth. And, of course, he must have known exactly why I was so anxious to return to the same town, the same hotel. And though he must have been dubious about that return, he booked us a room and again drove us, that July of 1973, toward the Atlantic Ocean.

At last I was sixteen. The magic age that Paul had told me the summer before might make me a contender for his affections. I was an incoming, heat-seeking missile, aimed solely at the heart of the love I had lost the summer before. Paul must have been aware of what was headed his way. Must have been thinking of an escape plan to use in a last-ditch bailout if one was called for. And, of course, one was.

I was set up on a date with Paul's younger brother, Andy, someone whom I almost certainly would never have dated left to my own devices. I tried to put a brave face on the situation and went out with him a couple more times during our week at the beach, but the truth is that I was devastated to have been rejected and handed over to his sibling like a castoff.

Rather than spending my days on a towel by the sea, I instead haunted a table on one of the hotel patios, writing tragic verse in a little notebook I carried with me, and trying to look both forlorn and careless at the same time. I longed for Paul to notice me, for I believed that if I could only catch his eye, his heart would be shaken by the brave and lonely portrait I made there in my flowered maxi dress, my long hair blowing in the ocean breeze.

Someone did notice me, but it was not Paul. And I did not find out about it until much later. Some months after my father died, in December of that same year, my mother told me, "Your Daddy was just heartbroken when he saw how hurt you were this past summer. He'd watch you out the window of our hotel room, sitting there alone, writing in your notebook, and it was almost more than he could bear."

"Really?" I had not thought my father was particularly aware of anything that had gone on with me during that week. The Watergate hearings were being televised that summer on national TV, and he spent every one of the sunny afternoons on the hotel bed, riveted. His loathing of Richard Nixon had been so vehement and all-consuming, I had assumed the rest of us were practically invisible.

"Oh, he was crushed by it," Mom said. "He never wanted to see you hurt by anything or anyone. He knew he couldn't do anything about it, and that was what bothered him so much."

This was a side of my father that I had not really known. Up until that time in my life, when boys became a compelling and incessant fixation, there had been little in my narrow world that had truly hurt me. The petty stings of childhood came and went, but they were always short-lived. And so this one summer, this heartache that colored what should have been a golden July, was the only occasion I knew of where my father had grieved for me.

*   *   *

But now, in the summer of 2013, Rehoboth Beach took on a new significance. When Chris and I went that year, it was hardly a relaxing getaway. With all of the ongoing research I was doing, and the various queries I had out to people and agencies far and wide, I couldn't afford to relinquish my connection to the internet for the four days we would be there. I have no iPhone, and the beach house we'd be staying in had no network I could access.

"I'm going to need to take my laptop over to that coffee house that has wifi—at least once a day," I told Chris.

He laughed. "Good thing I love coffee."

The weather during our stay was beastly hot, close to 100 degrees midday. The sand was scalding, so that even wearing flip-flops, the walk to where Chris and I would set up our beach umbrella scorched the winter-delicate skin of my feet. And yet each day we sat on the beach, Chris with a book to read and I with my research and a notebook.

All around us, teenagers laughed, parents reprimanded, children kicked up sand as they raced by, couples held hands, disc jockeys spun yet another tune. I might easily have annoyed any other man, one who wanted me to join him fully in the here and now, to lean over and kiss him in 2013. Fortunately, I had found the perfect partner in Chris. Instead of being irritated, he offered me another suggestion for the list, then leaned across his beach chair to kiss me somewhere between 1947 and 1951.

I was as happy as someone who didn't have answers to most of her questions could possibly be.

*   *   *

Home from the beach, I wrote again to my contact at the Archives to ask if he could give me any more information regarding her cause of death. Early on the morning of July 19, 2013, I received back the following response:

Dear Ms. McCabe:

This is in response to your recent inquiry to the National Archives concerning the death of Hazel E. McCabe.

The available documentation relating to the death of Hazel E. McCabe is available for review on Ancestry.com. The reasons for her death are explained in those records.[87]

My contact told me I needed to look for a specific file entitled REPORTS OF DEATH OF AMERICAN CITIZENS ABROAD, 1835-1974. I could then search for Hazel's name within that file.

What I discovered was beyond my wildest expectations.

As soon as I saw the first page of the document—discolored with age, stamped with dates, agency names, the quick scrawls in the margins of people who had written their commentary more than sixty years before – I had the eerie sensation of slipping backwards in time, of being trapped inside a tomb made of carbon paper and ghosts. The edges of many of the scanned pages were weighted down with little sandbags to keep the paper flat, the past pinned and labeled like a butterfly against a board. It felt as though I held my breath through the three hours it took to read through the nearly one hundred pages of the file.

The very first page bore my father's name. The heading at the top of the page read "Department of State—Memorandum of Conversation" and the date was February 27, 1951, just twelve days after Hazel's death:

Mr. McCabe called at the office concerning the death in Mexico on February 15, 1951 of Hazel Elizabeth White McCabe. Mr. McCabe stated that although he and Mrs. McCabe had been separated for some time, and while he had no responsibility technically, he did feel that he had a moral responsibility, and requested the Department's assistance in obtaining a report concerning the death of Mrs. McCabe.

Mr. McCabe first learned of the death of his former wife through a Mexican newspaper, which implied that the decedent had taken her own life. Mr. McCabe stated that although Mrs. McCabe had for some years taken barbiturates for sleeping, he felt reasonably sure that she was not capable of taking her own life. This statement was based on his knowledge of her temperament and the fact that he had been in communication with a number of her friends in the United States who had been in recent correspondence with her and who stated that her letters were cheerful and contained plans for the future.[88]

This memorandum posed all kinds of questions for me. How had Dad happened to be reading a Mexican newspaper? I wondered if maybe he was still trying to keep tabs on Hazel, and maybe that's why he kept in close contact with her friends. Which then made me wonder: was it only a moral obligation that led him to show up at the State Department, or was it because he was still in love with her?

Dad went on to request that if it were at all possible, "he would prefer that the official certificate of death did not indicate that she had taken her own life." There are a number of reasons Dad might have been motivated to ensure that the record did not imply that Hazel had committed suicide. He may have been acting out of concern for Hazel's posthumous reputation; but then, perhaps he worried that a death by suicide might stand in the way of a life insurance policy, if he was eligible to receive such a thing. I rejected that idea when I read the last sentence of the opening memorandum: "Mr. McCabe seemed quite upset over the death of his former wife and was particularly disturbed that no member of her family was present at the time of her interment."[89]

Dad's concern seemed genuine. From all I know and remember of my father, he had a tender and an empathetic heart. It would have hurt him profoundly to think that Hazel had been so depressed, so alone and hopeless, that she might have considered giving up on her life. I am sure that he must have asked himself if there had been anything he could have done to prevent this tragedy. Likely, he reviewed everything she had last said to him, everything that he had said in return. Had he said anything hurtful? Had he missed something in her mood or behavior that he might have done something about?

Dad had requested a report about Hazel's death, and within a month, this report was sent via the American Embassy in Mexico. Reading it myself, alone in my house on that July morning, I was shocked and saddened. As I made my way through the dry and factual report, I couldn't get out of my head the image of my father, sitting alone in the apartment where he then lived, on Q Street in D.C., reading these same words. They upset me, and I had never known this woman. I can't imagine what they would have done to him.

> The Embassy learned of the death of Mrs. Hazel Elizabeth McCabe from the Seventh Police Delegation and from Mr. Sam Bern who lives at Toledo 13, Apt 303, of this city. The latter stated that he and his wife had made Mrs. McCabe's acquaintance in New York some years ago and had not seen her again until they came to Mexico; that because of their former friendship they had visited each other frequently. Mr. Bern said that Mrs. McCabe began to drink heavily and that since he and his wife felt more or less morally responsible to look after her, Mrs. McCabe had given them the key to her apartment so that they could come in to see how she was getting along because she was in bed and under the influence of liquor most of the time.[90]

It was in this report that I would first learn the name of Sam Bern, the man I would go on to search for at length.

Bern characterizes Hazel as a dissolute drunk, lying about in bed all day, a far cry from the lively redhead remembered by so many of the people I had talked to. Perhaps this drastic change was in some way related to losing the court case she had pursued for so many years. Or perhaps her state was even related to her breakup with my father.

The report continued, "On the day of Mrs. McCabe's death, Bern said that he had called on Mrs. McCabe at 1 p.m., again about 7 p.m., and at 9:00 in the evening when he found her dead. Apparently he was the last one to see her alive at 7 p.m." This information seemed very strange to me. Why was Sam Bern checking on her so frequently? If she was in such a bad state emotionally, why hadn't some action been taken beyond simply popping in and out of her apartment? And why was it always Mr. Bern who did the checking, and not Mrs. Bern? My imagination ran wild.

> The police records reveal that Mrs. McCabe lost her life by taking an overdose of Seconal red capsules. There were still two or three in her hand when she was found dead. The physician, knowing how many capsules were in one of the bottles, assumed that she may have taken about forty of them.

> There is no way of knowing whether Mrs. McCabe took the sleeping pills with the intent of taking her life since Mr. Bern claims that she had been taking them consistently for a long period and that he had noticed that she had been increasing her dosage during the past few weeks.[91]

I thought it very odd that Sam Bern had such an intimate knowledge of Hazel's pill-taking habits. Why would he be monitoring exactly how many pills she took each day? If he were so concerned about her, why had he not intervened in some way?

This page of the file concluded on a fascinating note: "Her remains were cremated and shipped to her father in San Luis

Obispo, California." And so it happened that the man who had given Hazel up very shortly after her birth was to have her returned to him after her death.

Just when I thought the report could not get any more mystifying, I moved on to find a message sent from the Embassy to the State Department about a month later, in April of 1951. At some point during the moving of Hazel's effects from storage, in anticipation of their being shipped to her father, a wristwatch and a ring which had been among these effects had been stolen. After what seemed to me a rather cursory police investigation and search for the missing items, it was determined that nothing remained to be done but to determine the value of the ring and watch so that the executors of her estate (of whom one was her father) might be reimbursed for their value. The two pieces were described as "one Eska gold watch, with two stones, apparently good, one on each side of the face of the watch, held by a gold bracelet; and one white gold or platinum ring with engraved initials which cannot be read."

I also found a list of items that had been removed from her apartment after her death. The effect of reading through this was eerie, as though I had somehow stolen into her home and pawed through her closets and drawers. Nothing in the list was especially remarkable, but with each of the items mentioned, I felt I had more of a sense of who this woman might have been. Among the items in the long list were "19 dresses of different colors of silk and wool," "1 *rebozo*, woolen, white," (a *rebozo* being a long flat garment used by women, mostly in Mexico), "1 pair of slippers, flower design, green," "1 camera, Kodak, duplex, without case," "2 gold-plated necklaces," "2 silver brooches," and "miscellaneous papers and correspondence."[92]

How I coveted that last item— her miscellaneous papers and correspondence! What might I learn if all of those letters and papers were in front of me at that moment? They must have been sent to her father.

On June 11, 1951, Hazel's father Frank wrote a letter to the American Consulate in Mexico, replying to a letter they had sent him about Hazel's effects. In it, they had mentioned the stolen watch and ring, which clearly Frank was hearing about for the first time. He seems justifiably upset. He refers to the ring as a diamond ring and requests that they immediately send him word about the situation.

Over the ensuing months, a blizzard of paper swirled between Frank and the Embassy, Frank and the State Department, and the State Department and Mexico. Frank was getting more and more agitated about what seemed to him to be a failure of the State Department to compensate Hazel's estate for the loss of her jewelry. The estate hired an attorney to handle the negotiations back and forth. Frank and the attorney contended that the value of the ring and the watch was $736, but the bureaucrats at State were working hard to get a far lower estimate of their worth. Ultimately, the whole matter would be settled for $150, but it took nearly two years for this agreement to be reached.

In an attempt to get a lower appraisal of the jewelry than the $736 price, one of the State Department employees had the clever idea of contacting my father. After all, he reasoned, Dad had been married to her for many years and might be familiar with the pieces. The State Department employee wrote:

> The decedent's former husband lives in Washington and has from time to time been in touch with us since Mrs. McCabe's demise. Notwithstanding that he has no legal responsibility, he has always seemed anxious to be helpful. The thought occurred to our Miss Rock that he might remember the missing watch and ring, and be able to supply information of assistance in deflating the excessive claim of the McCabe executors.[93]

The letter goes on to state that Dad was contacted, and he mentioned that he and Hazel had made a careful inventory of all of their possessions when they had separated. He said he would look for this and be back in touch. He called back the very next morning. Clearly, he had spent the evening looking for the information they sought. I am sure he thought he was being of help, not to the State Department, but to Hazel's father and, consequently, to Hazel.

Far more interesting to me than the possible value of the jewelry was one letter in the file from a Walter E. Kneeland, who had been present during the transfer of the jewelry to the embassy. What he shared was startling, and cast new light on the involvement of Sam Bern in the night of Hazel's death:

> I first saw these articles on the night of Mrs. McCabe's death when a police officer and I accompanied Mr. Sam Bern to his apartment after he had been ordered to deliver this jewelry to the police authorities of the Seventh Delegation [...] Bern had improperly removed these valuables upon entering Mrs. McCabe's apartment and finding her dead.[94]

In another letter, written to the McCabe estate attorneys from the American Embassy, W. K. Ailshie, an official of the U.S. Embassy in Mexico, states:

> With regard to your inquiry as to how the fair value of this jewelry may be determined, I know of only four persons who saw it after Mrs. McCabe's death. These were Mr. Sam Bern, a friend of the deceased, who, upon entering her apartment and finding her dead, officiously removed this jewelry and other valuables to his home for safekeeping; Mr. Ignacio Funes Pontones, Agent for the District Attorney, who had Bern arrested for the unlawful removal of this property and for questioning; Counsel Walter E. Kneeland who intervened in the case as Protection Officer; and Mr. E. C. Rockefeller, an employee of this embassy who had custody of these articles at the time they were lost.

Bern has not been seen in town lately and it is presumed
that he has returned to his home in the United States.[95]

I had so many questions I didn't know where to begin.

*   *   *

Looking for new ways to delve into Mexico City in 1951, I sent
a message to a writer friend to ask him for his advice regarding
the hiring of a Mexican detective to do some digging for me. In
his own research, he had hired a detective to do some similar
work for him in Peru. He recommended to me that I look up
the World Association of Detectives, a reputable organization
that closely monitored and scrutinized the detectives who were
associated with them.

I looked on their site and found a detective named Fernando
Molina who was located in Mexico City. I sent him an email to
inquire whether he thought any of the records associated with
Hazel's death and Sam's arrest might still be found in police
records or Embassy files. By the next morning, Mr. Molina had
written me back:

Dear Ms. McCabe,

Those records could be archived or could be destroyed
already, unfortunately to know if they could exist we
require at least 8 hours of research. After that research we
could know if there is a chance to find those records.

Cost for research: $320.00 USD (prepaid).

If you are interested we will send you an invoice with
payment details and instructions.

The oldest record we have found was also in Mexico City
from 1926.

Yours truly,

Fernando Molina[96]

I was a bit leery about shelling out money for work that hadn't been accomplished yet, or to a man I knew virtually nothing about. I wrote him back, thanking him for his reply, but asking how he determined the eight-hour requisite for the research, and also inquiring how much he would charge me if he found the information I was seeking.

I never received a reply, even after sending a follow-up email. I suppose I had irritated him by questioning him. I was likely better off for not having hired him, but I still needed to find a detective.

I found another name online, but after I wrote to him, this guy turned me down at the outset, explaining that he was located four hours from Mexico City. He also indicated that it would be highly unlikely that the files would have been retained.

I couldn't find any other names online that looked even remotely reputable. I would have to go at this from another direction.

I could not get Sam Bern out of my mind. And I could not stop wondering about Hazel's last night.

Some time later, I started emailing with Arlene, a librarian at the Library of Congress. I told her about Hazel's death in Mexico, how I had found the State Department files on Ancestry, and had wondered what might have appeared in the Mexican papers. I knew at least one article had, because my father had apparently learned of her death from such an article. She ordered me micro-film from four different Mexico City newspapers from February, 1951, and I threaded the film into the viewer and began scrolling through the columns of text.

I am by no means fluent in Spanish, but after many years of study, I can certainly read it. Maybe not every word, but I was confident that I would get the gist of it if I found something. I scrolled and searched for her name, for the word *muerte*, the word *policia*, but not really believing that I would actually suc-ceed. She died late at night on the 15th of February. I began with the 16th and found nothing. But then, several pages into the

February 17th issue of *El Nacional*, I froze, blinked, and enlarged the picture. There was her name! And here at last was the story.

That day in the Newspaper Reading Room of the Library of Congress, I found three articles that covered Hazel's death. I thought I had known all the details about that night from the State Department report, but I was wrong. And most unsettling to me were the variations in the accounts given of the event by Sam Bern, the man who reported her death.

According to the article from *El Nacional*, entitled "*Misteriosa Muerte de Agraciada Dama*" or "The Mysterious Death of a Gracious Lady," Hazel's body was discovered in her bed with two unopened letters, addressed to her, and on the bedside table were two glasses, one holding water, the other, liquor, and a bottle of Seconals, with only one capsule remaining.

Upon questioning, Sam Bern told the police that he had met Hazel in New York and that they had become close friends. He said that Hazel had visited often with him and his wife, and that she was in the habit of drinking to excess; she had mentioned often that she wanted to die. She had become ill, and he would visit her every day. Just the day before her death, he visited her, finding her in bed. He said she had been lying there several days without leaving the apartment, and that she had complained bitterly that she had lost a probate case in Detroit amounting to $40,000.

Bern said he tried to console her, telling her not to worry, that really, she had lost nothing because she had never had that money, but that she was not satisfied and continued to complain.

According to this article's account, Bern said he returned to check on her that night, and believing her to be asleep, he sat down next to her to read. But then he noticed she was quite pale, and he touched her forehead, finding it freezing cold. Frightened, he ran out and told the building concierge that she was dead.

He told the police that he was sure she had committed suicide because she was "a neurotic" who continually said that she wanted to die. The article concluded by stating that, until the cause of death had been verified, Bern would be detained.[97]

For me, all of this new information served only to confuse Sam Bern's role in Hazel's life. If Hazel really was constantly proclaiming that she wanted to die, why was no psychiatric help sought for her? When Bern visited her on the night of her death, why was he pulling up a seat to read by what he believed to be her sleeping body? Was there not something rather odd about this behavior?

Excited by my discovery of this article, I grabbed another microfilm reel, this one from the Mexican newspaper, *Excelsior*. Barely daring to hope that I might get lucky again, I scrolled through the February 17th issue. And incredibly, there I found a second article: "The Strange Death of the American, White-McCabe." The opening of the article phrased the cause of her death in a sensational way, calling it "an apparent poisoning," and the police detective, Gonzalo Hernandez Zanabria, was reported to have said that he suspected Bern knew more than he would say about Hazel's death.

This article echoed many of the facts of the first one but phrased Bern's reporting of Hazel's suicidal thoughts in a strange way. Here Bern says that Hazel was attracted to, even beguiled by, the idea of death as though it were some sort of siren song that she had to follow.

This article also added to the story of Bern's first acquaintance with Hazel in New York. Here he stated that Hazel had told him she was thinking of visiting Mexico, and that she and Sam had decided to meet there.

Bern's account is more detailed here, stating that he tried to get her to go out to get something to eat, but that she did not want to. She asked him for a little rum with water, and he got it for her, and told her that he would return later. When he returned, he found her dead. There is no mention here of sitting down to read beside her body.[98]

I reached for the third microfilm reel with a great deal of excitement. The librarian, Arlene, had suggested to me that I try this newspaper, *Universal Grafico*, because it was a bit more on the sensational side, akin to something like our *National Enquirer*, and because it would contain photos.

Apparently *Universal Grafico* scooped the competition because I found a report of Hazel's death on February 16, a day before the other two accounts had appeared. When my scrolling through the reel at last came upon the article, I cried out with shock. Patrons of the Library of Congress turned and stared at me, and I instinctively covered my mouth with my hand. Yes, there were photos in this newspaper. And what had so shocked me was a close-up photo of Hazel's face after she had died.

What I felt was not only shock, but also pity. Whatever heartache this woman had caused my father, whatever negative remarks she had made to people about him, I have come to feel for her a kind of tenderness, a sympathy, that made me hurt for her at this affront to her privacy, this stripping away of her dignity. Did my father ever see this photo? Did it make him feel the same way that I felt?

The article leads with a subhead, stating that it was not yet known whether her death was a suicide or if a crime had been committed. It appeared that the question of whether or not a crime had occurred was the reason for Sam Bern's interrogation by the police.

Bern's account is somewhat different in this article. He informed the detective that he and Hazel had met in New York through a stockbroker, and that it was actually Bern's wife with whom Hazel was close friends. He is reported as saying that Hazel began to feel ill that night, and that he and his wife called a doctor, but that when the doctor arrived, Hazel was already dead. This account was at odds with the other two accounts. His wife had not been mentioned in the other articles.[99]

This revelation seems to contradict my communications with Bern's daughter, which indicated that his wife, Loretta, had no memory at all of Hazel. I have thought a lot about this. There are many events and people in our pasts that we might well be inclined to forget, but it does seem to me that one would not easily forget a friend who died in this tragic way, nor would one forget the night when one's husband was detained by the police for questioning. I don't know what to make of this: either Sam Bern concealed the extent of his involvement from Loretta, or she had no desire to recount her memories to me, a stranger. That I can certainly understand.

Sam Bern was released by the police after his interrogation. He was not held for any crime. They had no proof of any wrongdoing on his part. In all likelihood, Mr. Bern was not guilty of anything criminal. Immoral, maybe. But nothing illegal.

And yet. At bare minimum, Hazel needed help, an intervention of some kind, and not merely a friend to look in on her periodically to observe her drinking and drugging herself to death. That night in Mexico City, she did not have such a friend.

*   *   *

I've imagined Hazel's last day many times.

The radio is on in the bedroom, turned up loud. Not a station from el Distrito Federal, but a powerful station from San Antonio, Texas. Tonight, she will not listen to mariachis, to Big Band from the Hotel Reforma, but only to the Hit Parade from home.

She pours another scotch and weaves back and forth in the kitchen to Patti Page's "Tennessee Waltz."

I remember the night and the Tennessee Waltz
Only you know how much I have lost
Yes, I lost my little darlin' the night they were playing
The beautiful Tennessee Waltz.

The kitchen is small, but she circles it in waltz-time, stumbling a little, catching herself on the counter. The song is so schmaltzy, but every time she hears it, her eyes fill, her nose stings. It's that one damned line—"Only you know how much I have lost."

This is a song she should sing. Somewhere. If someone would pay her to sing again. She could really sell this song. Who else had lost so many in so short a time? Grandparents gone. Mother gone. And Terry.

She feels dizzier and takes a sip of her drink. She will skip dinner. Nothing in the apartment anyway, and too tired to go out. Had she missed lunch as well? She sees her reflection in the window against the darkness and then quickly looks away.

Mona Lisa, Mona Lisa, men have named you,
You're so like the lady with the mystic smile,
Is it only 'cause you're lonely they have blamed you?
For that Mona Lisa strangeness in your smile?

No one really knows her anymore. No matter how many nights she goes out with friends, dances in the arms of dark-haired men who ask her, she is far away from them. Like she is watching them from another room. Or the ceiling. Like she is floating. Like she can see her own body living life without her.

How long has it been since she went out anywhere? She isn't sure even which day it is. The weekdays blur without a job to go to. She will have to get a job soon. Who will she ask about that? Didn't someone somewhere tell her something—about a band that had lost its singer? Who was it?

Suddenly, she feels tired, too tired to stand up anymore. She pours more scotch into her glass and carries it to the bedroom, spilling only a little. She crawls into the bed, pats under her pillow to make sure her pills are still there. She won't take them yet. Or maybe she will take just a few, to make it easier to fall asleep when the time comes.

She puts them on her tongue, then chases them with the scotch. She looks at the clock. 6 p.m. Too early to go to sleep. She takes another sip and turns the radio lower. Don't get too drunk in case Sam comes back again. He checks on her too much. He won't leave her alone. She should never have given him that key. But it seemed a good idea at the time. And he had pushed so.

He had come by already today at 1 p.m., before she had gotten up and had assumed she had gone back to bed for a nap. She had stretched languorously beneath the thin sheet, propped herself up on one elbow so that a breast was almost completely exposed. She saw him notice. But he didn't try to touch her. She knew, though, that he would come back later.

She dozes, hears the key turning in the lock, and then a man's voice. "Hello?"

She opens her eyes, or tries to. It is so hard. Everything is heavy—her eyelids, her arms, her tongue. She should call out to him, but she can't seem to make her mouth move. Her lips dream the shapes of sounds, but do not make them.

"Hazel, are you okay?" Sam asks. He leans over her, gently rests his fingertips on her hand.

She wills herself to make sound. "Yes."

"Did you take your medicine?"

For a moment, she worries that she has left her pill bottle out where he can see it. She glances at the nightstand and sees only her half-empty tumbler of scotch and the clock that reads 7 p.m. She looks at her gold Eska watch. It is slightly off. The minute hand hovers just shy of the 12.

She nods.

"How many did you take?"

She smiles and holds up three fingers.

"No more now," Sam says. "That's too many, and you've been drinking." He moves backward out of the room. "I'll come back. After dinner. To see if you're okay."

She hears the click of the door, and blinks, letting the tears run down into her ears. She reaches under the pillow, pulls out the pills and spills a cascade of them out over the sheet. She has to sleep. She is so tired.

There is enough scotch left in the glass. She puts a few more on her tongue and swallows. And then she does it again. The radio is still on, and Sammy Kaye is singing.

*   *   *

I looked at the short vignette I had created. It might be true. At least parts of it might be true. But it wasn't good enough, simply to imagine.

I had struggled to try to understand what Hazel's last night might have been like. One night at dinner, I shared my frustration with another writer.

"I want so much to write this story," I told him. "But there are just too many things I don't know. All I have are questions. And speculations."

"Then why don't you try writing it as fiction?" he asked me. "Then you can write your own answers to the questions."

I shook my head emphatically. "No."

Since I began this quest back in May, nothing had been more important to me than finding out the truth. Yes, I could write this fantasized tale about what happened on the night of February 15, 1951, but this would not appease me. It was only a stopgap. A time filler.

I would not be able to write this story until I could tell it as it really happened.

I owed it to my father. And strangely, I felt I owed it also to Hazel.

William McCabe (Dad's father), Cyrus McCabe (Dad's grand-father), Dad, and Bob. Superior, Wisconsin. Circa 1918.

Dad. College. Early 1930s.

Frank White, Hazel's father. 1910. (Courtesy of Lory White Campagna)

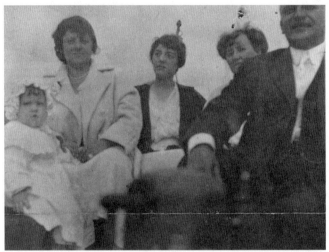

The Kramer family with baby Hazel. (Courtesy of The National Archives, Chicago)

Young Hazel with her grandparents. (Courtesy of Sumner Bagby)

Hazel's aunt, Hazel M. Kramer Bagby. (Courtesy of Sumner Bagby)

Hazel's childhood home in Saint Louis. (Courtesy of Sumner Bagby)

Tom and Edwina Williams with young Hazel, circa 1923. (Courtesy of Harvard Library)

I am very sure that this is a photo of young
Tom Williams, probably somewhere around
1935, found in Hazel's photo album.

Dad and the ladies of Alpha Omicron Pi, Hazel's sorority. Madison, WI.

Hazel performing her Mae West songs
at the 770 Club. Dad accompanies her
on the piano. University of Wisconsin,
Madison. 1934.

Florence, Hazel's mother, with Dad and Hazel on their wedding day.

A photo of Hazel and Dad that I believe was taken by Tom
Williams, in a hotel room, that night they spent together in
La Salle, 1937.

Photo of Hazel, taken by Dad, most likely on their honeymoon.

Another photo of Hazel captured by Dad, around the time of their honeymoon.

Formal portrait of Hazel and Dad, recently after their wedding day.

Hazel with her mother and grandparents.

Dad with Hazel's family.

Florence in her car, which was referenced in Williams' short story "Three Players of a Summer Game."

Written across the bottom of the cardboard frame are the words: "Don't think it hasn't been fun. Romayne '43-June 27. My eleventh post-operative day and I feel like a million bucks. Hazel."

Caricature of Dad. Hung in his office throughout my childhood.

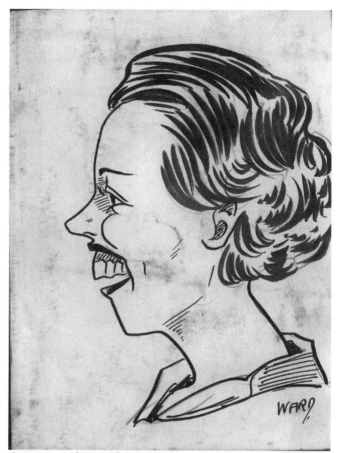

Caricature of Hazel from college.

Russell Henderson Burke, the mysterious beneficiary in Hazel's will. (Courtesy of Yale Library)

Dad and Mom.

Dad and Mom on their wedding day.

Dad with me and my sister, Terri.

McCabe Family Portrait, 1971.

Mom, Terri, and me, 1975.

Terri and me, right after her diagnosis.

Hazel's last formal portrait before her death.
(Courtesy of Lory White Campagna)

FAMILIES, DESTROYED AND REPAIRED

Prompted by his unexpected appearance after Hazel's death, I went looking for Frank M. White, the elusive father, the man who gave her away and then seemingly disappeared.

Online I found an obituary for a Katherine Quinn, no one to me but for the name given of her first husband, Franklin Madison White, Jr. Surely this junior was the son of the man I was searching for. Hazel's father had lived in California; this Katherine Quinn had lived in California, too. And here were the names of all four of their children, and the towns that held their lives.

Hazel was their father's half-sister. Had he known her? Had any of them ever met their Aunt Hazel? Or had Frank Sr. kept her a secret always, held her at a remove, unwilling to let the past enter the life he had made in this warm world so far away from Missouri?

I uncovered addresses for all four of the children, wrote a letter and included a photo of my father with Hazel, both of them young and hopeful and in love. Dropping each envelope into the mailbox outside the post office felt like casting a fishing line into the opaque surface of a lake.

First I received an email from Raymond White, grandson of Hazel's father. Yes, he told me. I had found them. They knew about their Aunt Hazel, though I quickly learned that some of what they knew was skewed. He believed that she had died in Mexico in an automobile accident, the same story that had been told to my cousin, Roberta, on my father's side. Raymond sent me a photograph taken in 1950 of his grandmother, Frank Sr.'s second wife, next to a woman he believed might be Hazel. I could see immediately that he was mistaken. The woman in the photo was well into her fifties; she was heavy-set with thick ankles and deep furrows in her face. I looked back at the photo I have of Hazel smiling from a restaurant table in 1943. There was no way this open, unlined face and slender frame could have altered so drastically in only seven years.

That evening, I received an email from Raymond's youngest sister, Lory. She was surprised and excited to hear from me. She had a photograph that she knew was her Aunt Hazel. She told me she would hunt for it and send it to me.

I sent her the restaurant photograph from 1943. You might not be able to tell from this black-and-white photograph, I wrote to her, but Hazel was a redhead. She wrote back that no, she could not tell it from the photo I sent, but that the photograph she would send me was in color—that I would plainly see her red hair.[100]

I would soon learn that most of the White family members were redheads. These were indeed Hazel's people.

*   *   *

Lory sent me the photo, a color snapshot of Hazel in a raincoat, standing near some flowers, her red hair loose, her curls windblown. She looked a bit older than the photos in my possession, and the picture was very small and difficult to make out, but I could still see that it was her. Had her father taken this photo? Was the smile she offered up to the camera lens for Frank? Had she so readily forgiven him for his desertion, for his disappearance from her life when she was just a baby? Or was there nothing to forgive? Perhaps she had never blamed him for any of it. Perhaps her child's mind had created a story that absolved him.

In her message to me, Lory wrote about Hazel, "My mother had told me that she had taken her own life before I was born."[101] So not everyone had been told an invented tale of her death. Lory's father, who was Hazel's half-brother, and his wife had known the truth.

Lory also sent me a small photograph of Frank, so small that I could barely discern the features of his face. The one thing the photo did show plainly was that he was quite tall. At last I understood where Hazel's long, willowy body had come from.

In later emails, Lory sent additional photographs. There is one taken of the entire family at Lory's older sister Karen's baptism. Here Hazel stands in the exact center of the group, the baby Karen in her arms. Clearly she had been absorbed into the White family. It made me feel strangely happy for her. All of her Kramer family had died by then, except for the aunt with whom she did battle over her grandmother's will. She and my father had parted ways. I was glad that she had not been alone.

Later still, Lory sent me a large color portrait of Hazel in an olive-green dress, her red curls especially vivid, her lips painted an even darker red. Along with this she sent two formal portraits of Frank. At last I could see his features plainly. Here indeed was the parent Hazel resembled. I wondered if it had ever bothered Florence to see how much her daughter looked like the husband who may well have left her for another woman.

*   *   *

In *The Distant Hill*, Dad included a passage where Florence recalls the demise of her marriage and Lizbeth's adoption:

Mrs. Kemmerer gasped and her hand went quickly to her pounding heart. Slowly she caught her breath, but the memories Lizbeth's flat statement called forth were brought back in indelible clarity to her mind. The picture she saw of Jim coming to see his wife and baby and being refused admittance by her father; the sound of the pen as Jim only half-consciously scratched his name on the adoption papers, the tears that fell unnoticed and made the signature run in a blue stream until the clerk so quickly blotted it up.

I found this passage intriguing for a number of reasons. I knew from my research that Florence was not present when her husband Frank and her parents signed the adoption papers. So Florence *Kramer* could never have had this memory. But it started me thinking about where Dad had come up with this anecdote. One would think it had come from Hazel, but obviously, it could not have been an event that she had witnessed either. And it did not seem at all likely that her grandparents would have passed on a tale that made her father seem full of regret for having signed away his daughter.

It was not until I finally got access to the testimony from the trial that I began to make sense of this. In 1939, Hazel and Dad had looked up Hazel's father, Frank M. White, in New York, where he was then practicing law. What a surprise it must have been for him to receive an unexpected phone call from his now-grown daughter. And how anxious Hazel must have felt, walking into that office and seeing her father for the first time. Perhaps my father had suggested to her that she go alone, that it should be a very personal and private moment, and Hazel had begged him to accompany her. I can understand that reaction, if it were true. It was an unsettling and scary undertaking she had set out on; she likely wanted my father's support as she entered a situation where she would not know what to expect.

It must have been Frank, then, that gave this account of the adoption day. It is an account quite at odds with the one that Emil apparently shared with my grandfather. In Emil's account, Frank could scarcely wait to sign the papers and be free of his financial obligation to this little girl.

The fact that my father attempted to render the adoption scene as Frank remembered it, coupled with the fact that my cousin Roberta had been told the same story about Hazel's death as Raymond White, makes me think that my father and Frank were at least acquaintances. I have imagined that Dad accompanied Hazel when she went to meet Frank for the first time. Moreover, the report from the National Archive revealed that my father wrote to Frank following her death. He wanted to make sure Frank knew that Hazel had once expressed her desire to be interred next to her mother. This is why Hazel's ashes are now in St. Louis, and not in California where they had been originally shipped. Whether Dad and Frank knew each other well or not, it seems that they were united by a mutual love for her. I believe that in her last few years, Hazel saw the Whites as her family. This gives me some small comfort in this often morbid investigation: that even as Hazel became further estranged from the Bagbys and the Kramers, she still had people who wished her well.

*　　　　*　　　　*

The case, McCabe v. Bagby, that I had first stumbled upon online years ago, had proven to be very difficult and expensive to obtain. I enlisted the help of my attorney friend, Annie; I made numerous phone calls that bounced me all over the Midwest; I paid a hefty copying fee, and ultimately was sent what I thought would be the case that I had sought for so long. The day that all 300+ pages of it were delivered to my door, I sat down and read it beginning to end. My glee slowly changed to disappointment as I realized that what I had spent so much energy and money for was not the actual court case, at all. There was plenty in it that was interesting, but it was not the trial I had read about online. Instead, it had to do with the probate of Emma's will.

What it did offer to me was tantalizing, however. In addition to a list of people who were deposed, a list that included Tennessee Williams' mother, I also came upon a point-by-point complaint of the case that Hazel was making against her aunt, Hazel Bagby. Here was Hazel's story of what had happened, and it did not portray Mrs. Bagby in a flattering light.

The complaint laid out the story of her parents' divorce and her adoption by the Kramers. According to this document, Hazel's father, Frank, was induced to agree to the adoption because of the Kramers' promises to give Hazel every advantage and to assure her, upon their deaths, a share in their estate that was equal to that of their other two daughters. Moreover, Frank would be absolved of paying any kind of alimony or child support. To secure this arrangement, Frank must promise to forfeit all contact with his daughter.

After the death of Hazel's mother, Florence, in 1943, Hazel had received the entirety of Florence's estate, but according to the adoption arrangement, she was still to receive a third of her grandmother, Emma's, estate. (Her grandfather Emil had died in 1942.)

At this time, the complaint maintained, "Hazel M. Bagby induced said Emma Kramer to leave her home in St. Louis and to come to live in Birmingham, Michigan, and to live in the house of said defendant [...] Thereafter, said Emma Kramer's health rapidly failed, and from the time of her removal to Birmingham until the time of her death (at which time she was upwards of eighty years of age) the defendant Hazel M. Bagby, by solicitation, blandishments and persuasion induced said Emma Kramer to give her large sums of money amounting to at least $40,000 and to transfer sundry bank accounts and securities to the joint names of herself and Emma Kramer, all in an effort to obtain more than her agreed upon share of the property of said Emil J. Kramer and Emma Kramer."[102]

Hazel's complaint went on to claim that her aunt had manipulated Emma's mind against her granddaughter, the result of which was that Hazel's portion of the estate had been reduced to a paltry $1,000, while all the rest of it went to Hazel Bagby, and her sons, John and Walker.

The probate case also provided me more than 40 pages of testimony from Hazel Bagby herself. She talked about my father, intimating that her parents had not been all that keen on him. And she made many remarks which supported the picture of her sister, Florence, that my father had painted in *The Distant Hill*: a woman given to temper tantrums and fits of hysteria. She also, surprisingly, testified that she believed, despite everything, that she still loved her niece, Hazel.[103]

In reading this, I found myself confronted with a flesh-and-blood woman instead of the sinister figure I had dreamed up in my own mind. What did I know about Hazel Bagby and who she really was? Nothing, really. Nothing that wasn't conveyed to me through a skewed lens, a dark picture developed in the courtroom by Hazel's attorney. She had spirited Emma out of St. Louis to live with her in Michigan, sequestered her and kept her from receiving letters, influenced her and colored her view of her granddaughter, filled her with false ideas, coerced her into changing her will, all but cutting off her young niece without a dime.

How much of this was an accurate portrayal of who this woman was? I had only one side of the story to go on, and in the absence of disputing claims, I colored in her outlines in black. I made her into the villain of the story.

I set out to find the Bagbys with a bit of trepidation. After all, I was telling the story of the woman who had challenged a will that left them all a great deal of money, had dragged them into court, caused them enormous stress and embarrassment, and had consumed their lives for several years. Surely whatever family love had once existed had been all but eradicated by this strife and unrest.

A bit of research via Ancestry and Google, and I had the name of a man I believed to be Hazel Bagby's grandson, now in his sixties. Would I find him on Facebook? Yes, indeed, I would. I set out to craft a message that would accomplish a number of aims: assure him that I was a credible human being and not some crackpot, intrigue him with my knowledge of his family's history, and refrain from giving even the merest hint that I thought of his grandmother as someone who had caused my father's first wife heartache and trouble.

I waited for a reply that never came. Instead, after a week or so, I received a message from his wife, telling me that yes, I had found the right person, but that her husband really knew very little of his family history. If I wanted to speak to family members who really knew a lot, I should get in touch with his sister, Nancy, and his cousin, Cindy. She provided me with contact information.[104]

And so I had an email address for Cindy, but all I had for Nancy was a phone number with a D.C. area code. She was close to me. But I did not want to cold-call this woman out of the blue and force her to have to deal with me, whether she wanted to or not. The truth was, I was afraid. I was the last remaining representative of the "enemy camp." It was easier to approach through email, where I could craft a message that took its time, that clarified and reassured, that gave the recipient an opportunity to digest all the sudden information before having to reply. I wrote an email to Cindy and then waited to see what would happen.

She wrote me back in just a couple of days. Her response surprised me. There was no guardedness, no cold reserve, no clipped response to my queries. She was warm, interested, and even grateful to hear that I was writing a book about her family.

She wanted to help me and readily agreed to identify photo-graphs and to send me copies from the Bagby family albums.

She also offered a surprising piece of information that I took as unlikely, a kind of family myth, but nonetheless, it started me wondering. She wrote, "I think there was a rift in the family after the problem with the will. My father never spoke well of T. Williams, I think because of his part in this. It was almost as if he blamed Tennessee for Hazel's actions, which of course I can't verify was really true! He never spoke ill of Hazel. I wonder if the family felt guilty about her suicide."[105]

What did she mean, Tennessee Williams' "part in this"? Of course, I knew that Hazel had written to Tom, asking for his written testimony about her relationships with family members. His letter in response seemed to have disappeared and had not been used in the actual trial, though I had not given up hope of finding it. But there was no evidence of any kind that Tom had involved himself any further in Hazel's legal battle. Could Cindy be right about this?

I wrote back that I was surprised by her remarks related to Williams and asked her if they were based on facts, or were just suppositions. She replied, "For some reason my father men-tioned Hazel and Tennessee in a big car—not sure why this is significant, but I have a strong memory of it. Not sure if my father felt this was important because it meant that T was help-ing Hazel financially or just providing emotional support. I always thought there was some financial support, but this could be my father's take on it. Anyway, I got the feeling my father deeply resented T's involvement. He probably felt it was none of T's business. As I said in another letter, he did not like T. I can imagine the frugal Bagbys thought the whole trial was a waste of money since breaking a will is so difficult."[106]

Meanwhile, Nancy was proving harder to contact. Although I had originally been given her phone number, I was very reluc-tant to use it. One can read an email, then mull it over, absorb it, and decide how to respond. But a phone call is a direct assault that offers no space to ponder and to consider, outside of rudely hanging up. Cindy eventually gave me her cousin's street address in D.C. and an email. I first tried the email, with no result. I would subsequently learn that she never used it. And so, at last, I wrote a letter to the home in D.C.

A week passed, and I was losing hope of hearing from her, when suddenly she called. I was surprised by her voice, so friendly and open, with the distinct Midwest twang that I was so used to hearing from my father's side of the family.

Unlike Cindy, Nancy did not seem to know anything about the trial. I filled her in on the basics. Her reaction to my revelation that after losing the case, Hazel had moved to Mexico and shortly thereafter, committed suicide, was startling and immediately endearing.

"Oh, I feel sort of guilty about this."

Of course, I countered this remark. What had she to do with all that had transpired? Who could know with any certainty what had motivated Hazel's final act?

"I still feel bad about it."

I instantly liked this woman. She was open and interested and seemed eager to offer me any assistance she could. She told me that she would be going to Michigan in July and would look through her parents' photos and memorabilia to see what she could find. She recalled some home movies that her father had kept; a box full of old reels, some of which had been shot of the family as far back as the twenties. She had "played" one of these for her Dad on one of his last birthdays—a scene of him at age five, blowing out his birthday candles.

He had pointed to a young woman at the table. "That's Hazel, my cousin."

Nancy had never seen her before.

"There were other people he mentioned," she told me. "I've forgotten the names."

But Hazel certainly was there, a young woman in the presence of a family she had once been so close to. Over the years, misunderstandings and disagreements would begin to drive a wedge between Hazel and her family. The rift these conflicts caused would eventually alienate her from her aunt, her cousins, and even her grandmother. These losses would weigh heavily on her in the last few years of her life.[107]

Hazel's Day in Court

I was in Chicago. In the dead-white iciness of winter.

I, who despise cold weather and who had always shivered at the mere idea of ever traveling to "The Windy City," had traveled there, willingly and utterly alone. I was not by nature prone to rash actions. But what I had previously known of myself had not incorporated this new and gnawing desire to understand what had happened all those many years ago to my father. My months-long pursuit of the court case that Hazel had instigated to overturn her grandmother's will had finally met with success; I had pinpointed my quarry, and that quarry was in a branch of the National Archives located in Chicago, Illinois. There was nothing to be done but to buy a plane ticket and go.

As I sat there at that long wooden table that morning, having landed just an hour before, I looked over the imposing stack of documents in front of me. I was so excited I was almost shaking. I had searched hard to track down this case, spurred on by the hope that it would provide answers to all the questions that were plaguing me. The Archives staff had stripped me of all of my possessions except a pad of paper, a pen, and a digital camera. My plan was to shoot images and read later, but I discovered that it was impossible not to be pulled into the story.

At the moment when I turned a page and unexpectedly saw my grandfather's name, the beginning of testimony I had not known would be there, I actually made a quick intake of breath so audible in that quiet, echo-prone room that all eyes turned toward me, including the vigilant librarian on staff.

I laughed and pointed to the page. "It's my grandfather!" I called out.

She seemed to relax. "I thought you had torn something."

*   *   *

That winter morning in Chicago, sitting with the entirety of McCabe v. Bagby before me, I left the present day behind me and let myself become immersed in what had happened in those early spring days 66 years ago.

It was April 1948, in Detroit, Michigan, and Hazel was at last having her day in court. She had staked a lot to arrive at this moment. That first morning, she must have felt tremendously anxious, but she was not alone as she began this battle against her aunt. Also in the courtroom with her was her father, Frank M. White; her dear friend, Ivy Jennings McNamara; and my own grandparents, her former in-laws.

Reading my own grandfather's testimony was a revelation to me. I had only the vaguest memory of a visit he and my grandmother had made to us when I was somewhere between three and four years old. He died when I was five. According to my mother, I was instantly attached to William McCabe, this former railroad engineer who was drawn each afternoon to walk along the railroad tracks at the bottom of our street, his hands clasped behind him, his head tipped down, his mind somewhere many decades and miles removed from our Virginia town in 1962.

"He took you with him," my mother told me. "Or rather, you tagged along, and he didn't say 'no.' What a sight the two of you made, walking down those tracks. This old man and this tiny girl, both with their hands clasped behind their backs, both lost in their own thoughts. You imitated everything he did."

In his testimony, my grandfather provided an enlightening picture of Hazel's grandparents and aunt, of what they likely thought of my father and his family, and of what they valued.

Grandpa met the Kramers and the Bagbys when everyone had come together to spend time at a summer cottage on Lake Mendota, the summer after Hazel and Dad had gotten married. My grandfather testified that on one evening, Emma had said to E.J., "Why don't you take Mr. McCabe out on the lawn and have a talk?" Clearly, this talk had been planned by the Kramers, and my grandfather probably had no idea what he was walking into.

He testified, "Quite abruptly he asked me if I owned any A&P stock. I told him that I did not. He inquired what kind of stock I did have, and I told him that I was never much in the market in that manner of purchasing stock and so forth. He wished to know what stock investments my son had. I told him I didn't know and had never made any inquiries into his financial dealings. He said, 'Everyone should own some stock. It gives them a sense of responsibility' and so forth. Quite abruptly, he said 'You know Hazel is our daughter, don't you?' and I said, 'Yes, I understood that she carried your name and you had adopted her when she was quite young.' He said, 'We have given her a home over a long period of time and educated her. We took her away from her fool of a father who didn't know enough to take care of anything he had given to him or had acquired, and now instead of having a no-good father, she stands to come into a goodly sum of money.' There was a little other discussion as to stocks and bonds and so forth."[108]

Later, Emma joined my grandfather and E.J. out on the lawn and added her voice to this strange conversation. Grandpa testified, "She said, 'You know we have had considerable trouble in our life, Mr. McCabe.' And I presume that I remarked that we all did, and then she said, 'I think that we have had more than our share. You know that we have taken Hazel McCabe as our daughter and have given her a good education, and Mr. Kramer and myself…worry a great deal. You know, Hazel and the other girls will come into considerable money.' She designated it as 'a pretty penny.' And she continued, 'We sometimes worry if they are going to be able to take care of it or not.'"[109]

My grandfather confided to the attorney questioning him that he had found this conversation a very uncomfortable one. "It was rather embarrassing to me to talk money," and so he tried to turn the conversation in another direction. But this would not be the only money-related conversation he had to submit to, visiting at this summer cottage. He also testified about meeting Hazel Bagby, and a discussion she had with him:

> She didn't seem to feel that my son had a job commensurate with his ability. […] She asked me what a change in the state administration would do for my son's betterment in employment. […] He was a statistician for the (Wisconsin) Department of Agriculture. […] Mrs. Bagby said she did not think the two children, Hazel McCabe and Terrence, were thrifty enough and did not have respect for money that they should have, and they perhaps were living a little beyond their means.[110]

Grandpa went on to say that Hazel Bagby told him she had a close connection who was an executive on the Southern Pacific Railroad, and she suggested to him that perhaps some wheels could be greased that would secure my father a better-paying job in the railroad industry. My grandfather joked that "very few fathers want their sons to follow their footsteps," and I am sure he was made just as uncomfortable by this conversation as he had been by the one with the Kramers.

Mrs. Bagby went on to say that Hazel had had a great deal of money spent on her, more than had been spent on Florence or herself. My grandfather also reported her saying, "my father was quite disappointed that your son hasn't a more stable disposition about money and Hazel also hasn't and very likely he will put it (the money he would leave to her) in a trust fund."

Though Mrs. Bagby's assessment of my father and Hazel's financial responsibilities seems consistent with what my cousin Roberta remembers about their lack of domesticity, somewhere along the passage of his life, my father certainly gained a strong appreciation for money, though he was by no means ruled by it. He was generous to a fault with presents and small, spontaneous purchases, but when it came to big expenses, such as cars or household appliances, he was very tight with his cash, and researched the purchases so painstakingly and extensively that it would drive my mother crazy.

I got my first taste of the importance my father placed on being able to earn a good income the day that I told him I wanted to be a writer when I grew up. I thought my choice would make him happy. After all, I had grown up to the sound of his 1939 Royal clacking away for many hours after I went to bed each night. He wrote every day, and as a child, I was aware that he was working on a book about his hometown of Superior that he hoped very much to get published.

However, he had a strong and negative reaction to my literary ambitions. He shook his head, clearly dismissive, almost angry, at my answer. "Nah, you don't want to be a writer." He shook his finger at me. "I'll tell you what you should be. An economist. Or a lawyer."

The field of economics had served my father well, and he earned a good living through his position with the Department of Agriculture. And I realize now that his past had given him plenty of exposure to lawyers, especially during those years when Hazel was contesting Emma's will and when she sought the dissolution of their marriage.

In retrospect, I understand that he wanted the best for me. He wanted me to be financially independent and successful. To his credit, he didn't suggest a stereotypically female occupation. He saw me going far, in what was then a man's world. But he had a very strong reaction against the idea of my being a writer. Though he had aspirations of his own, Dad always depended on his government job to keep us afloat. As a child, I had no real sense of how much money my father earned or had amassed over time. But after he died, what he left to my mother must have been considerable. Though my mother did not remarry for another thirteen years after Dad's death, she never had any need of getting a job to support us. Dad had provided her not only with enough for us to live on, but also ample to send both my sister and me through college without having to borrow a cent. Either something must have changed from the time that Hazel Bagby expressed her concerns to my grandfather, or her assessment of my father's relationship with money was colored by her own relationship with money.

Grandpa added to his description of the meeting with Hazel Bagby: "She mentioned considerable [sic] about her ability to take care of money and intimated that at least her husband was quite wealthy and quite capable of taking care of money and that her sons would come in for money from some other place."

It seemed to me that Hazel Bagby was conveying two things to my grandfather: first, that she was someone who could be depended upon to manage money wisely, and second, that any money that might go to her niece and my father would be frittered away.

The lawyer then asked Grandpa a question that almost caused me to cry out and risk another public disturbance in this quiet Archive. "Will you state whether or not the marriage of your son to Mrs. McCabe was recently annulled?"

My grandfather responded, "That is our understanding. […] She admits it and he tells me, so it must be true."[111]

Annulled! This was indeed a shock to me. Dad and Hazel had been married for twelve years. Neither of them was a Catholic. Why an annulment? I knew this was something I was going to need to pursue. But the lawyer had asked the question for a reason. He wanted to show that my grandfather had nothing to gain monetarily if Hazel succeeded in having the will overturned. Despite objections from Mrs. Bagby's attorney, Grandpa insisted on making a statement as to why he was there.

"May I make a statement so as to clear the confusion on this? I am coming here because of [...] what you might term 'injustice.' Although there is a change in the status of the family relationship [...] I don't feel [that] should change my consideration on this."[112]

Clearly, my grandfather felt that Hazel had been wronged, and he felt it was his duty to appear and tell what he knew. His integrity made me proud of him, as did his discomfort at the Kramer family's persistent focus on money.

After spending an entire day wading through hundreds of pages of testimony in the two court cases Hazel instigated after her grandmother's death, I came away feeling unclean and full of pity. After reading all of the evidence and statements of witnesses on both sides, it wasn't possible to know with certainty who was telling the truth, and who was not. I had my own theory, but perhaps both of the Hazels were telling the truth as they knew it, as they had fashioned it in their own minds.

But what left me saddened and even a bit disgusted was the avaricious excess of the whole time-consuming and family-destroying debacle. Such an immense battle waged over money when both women already had so much of it.

Emma had left an estate that was worth over $200,000 in 1947. Adjusting for inflation, this amount would be comparable to just over two million in 2017 dollars. It wasn't hard to see why Hazel might fight for her half of this legacy, and against what she perceived as injustice and underhanded tactics on the part of her aunt. I could also imagine why Hazel Bagby might have felt that most of this money should go to her, given that her niece had already received a generous legacy from Florence's estate: $85,000 in 1943, on top of many thousands more from her grandfather's will.

But the fight for this money came at an enormous cost. It divided a family, alienated Hazel from her grandmother and aunt, split apart cousins who had been fond of one another, and may well have contributed to her slide into alcoholism, drug abuse, and finally, suicide. It wasn't losing the money that devastated Hazel, I don't think. I think it was the slow and steady loss of all the people she had loved. Her support system had never been vast. Her family had been small. She lost her grandfather and then her mother over a two-year period, and then her grandmother had left to live with her aunt in Michigan. It seems that efforts Hazel made to contact them and visit in Michigan were rebuffed. And then, of course, she had ended the marriage with my father, for reasons I still felt I had yet to fully understand.

Hazel's second court case did, however, provide some insights. If the testimony of the witnesses can be believed, then Hazel seems to have grown up in a family for whom money was a constant fixation. One person after another testified that Emma had told them that one day, Hazel was going to be a very wealthy woman because of the Kramers' plan to divide their estate equally among the three daughters. Emma appears to have shared this information with numerous friends and neighbors, and even my own grandparents.

Emil seemed to show his love for his children through the purchase of stocks and bonds rather than any physical or verbal demonstrations. He had come from a very poor background, having lost his parents at an early age, and he had slowly struggled to make a success of himself. This hard-won affluence seemed to have created a fixation on the acquisition of wealth and the issue of who would receive this money after he and Emma died. Over the years, it would appear that the Kramers made many wills, amending them as soon as a new family development changed the inheritance landscape.

How much of this did Hazel absorb? Was money important to her as she grew up, or was it simply taken for granted? Surely she had not been chasing after money when she married my father, for in those Depression years, he had very little. But perhaps, the expectation she had of one day inheriting a third of a very sizable estate had made my father seem like a risk worth taking. Perhaps her discovery that Emma had left her with next to nothing had an influence on her decision to split with my father.

At some point, probably long after Hazel was gone, my father had invested extensively and wisely in the stock market. This was certainly not an endeavor he had been assisted in by his own father. From reading my grandfather's testimony from the court case, I knew Will McCabe had never attempted to buy stocks. He had indicated as much to Hazel's grandfather when questioned about it that summer in 1937. So where had my father acquired his stock market acumen? And how had he obtained the money for the original purchases that would end up providing my mother, sister and me such a generous cushion against financial hardship? I believe he must have received his market tutorial from Emil Kramer. Perhaps, as well, some purchase had been made for Hazel and my father, to help them get a start in their married life.

Clearly, the Kramers were dubious about my father being able to adequately support Hazel. Dad had ended up doing very well, but at the time of his marriage to Hazel, he must have seemed to the Kramers to be a very bad bet.

*　　*　　*

Despite her considerable efforts, the many witnesses Hazel's attorneys brought forth to testify in her behalf, and no doubt the significant amount of money she had put toward this challenge, the judgment went against her and in favor of the Bagbys. The plaintiff would "take nothing" and Emma's will would stand. This judgment was dated March 13, 1950. In less than a month, Hazel had filed an appeal.[113]

She would also lose the appeal but would not receive word of it until February of 1951, while she was living in Mexico. According to Sam Bern, her neighbor and seemingly closest contact in that city, this loss was what led her to take her own life with alcohol and pills. But I wasn't sure the answer was as simple as that.

For one thing, after months of effort, I had finally obtained a copy of Hazel's will. And the will raised new questions, not the least of which was the possibility that a failed love affair might have had as much to do with Hazel's death.

The Mystery Man

Who thinks about making a will when she is only thirty-seven years old? At that age, I had two daughters in elementary school who required a great deal of my focus, and I was running my own freelance business as an advertising copywriter. I certainly had no fortune to pass on. Though perhaps unwise, it never dawned on me to make a will.

What made Hazel so different from me? Just two months shy of her thirty-eighth birthday, she went to the offices of her attorney and made a will that bequeathed all that she owned to the various important people in her life. Was she simply a financially prudent person, one who had been well inculcated in the practice of will-making and estate-settling by the Kramers, who clearly had quite a penchant for it? Perhaps all the haggling and strife created by her challenge of her grandmother's will made Hazel a sadder but wiser woman when it came to inheritance. Perhaps she even feared that without one, all her money would go to the woman she now saw as her enemy: her aunt, Hazel Bagby.

Or had her father, Frank White, urged her to write a will? He was an attorney and so may well have advised her that this would be a prudent move. Were his motives selfless, or did he realize that if Hazel were to die intestate, he would never see a penny of her fortune? He had no legal family connection to her anymore, having permitted her to be adopted when she was just a baby. He certainly knew she was making one, as he was one of her executors. I had seen references to this in the National Archive file about her death, and it was how I knew to search for a will at all.

It took a lot of searching and more of my money paid once I located it in New York, but when I finally received the two documents—both the probate and the tax files—many months after my quest began, I realized that it was worth every penny.

The most obvious benefit to me was that I now knew the names of the people who were among her inner circle, the people about whom she felt strongly enough that she wanted to leave them money and/or possessions. I was not surprised to see her father, Frank, among the bequests, or her half-siblings, Frank Jr. and Gertrude. I was more surprised to find that she had left money to *my* father. Clearly, whatever had caused them to separate had not resulted in hostility or bitterness. Or maybe it had, but she wanted somehow to set things right. She left him $1,000, which in 1950 had the same buying power as $9,900 does now. It wasn't a goldmine, by any means, but it was not an insignificant sum. She left the same amount to many of her closest friends.[114]

The bequest that truly startled me—both for the amount of money bequeathed and for all that the total bequest implied— was to a man that I had never heard of, Russell Henderson Burke. Hazel had left him $10,000, her Dynaphone, her diamond ring, and all of her furniture. I had just acquired a new Mystery Man.

The day she signed that will, in September of 1950, Hazel had left this man what amounted to a small fortune. Ten thousand dollars then would be equivalent to just over $100,000 in 2017 dollars. It was double what she was leaving to her own father. And it was ten times as much as she left to my father, her former husband. Surely he must be someone of great significance to her. If he merited more than her own biological family, then surely he must be more than just a friend. I assumed immediately that this Mr. Burke must have been Hazel's lover. I had only to find a way to prove it.

I got only one hit when I went looking for "Russell Henderson Burke" on Google and Ancestry, but it proved to be of tremendous value to me. It was a link to a page from a 1925 Yale yearbook, and suddenly, there he was: a handsome, almost baby-faced young man, listed as being on the baseball and basketball teams, and having "prepared" at Exeter Academy. I contacted the Yale Alumni Association, which put me in touch with the keeper of Yale's Archives, and began an exchange of emails with them that would yield me a great deal of information. And with that information, I built a family tree for him on Ancestry that would lead me to even more knowledge.

I learned that he had been born in Chicago in 1902, as Russell Harry Carr, to a woman named Genevieve and a man named William H. Carr. The marriage did not last, and Genevieve and William divorced. Genevieve moved on, and by 1906, she was married to a man named Walter Burke, who would adopt Russell and give him his name.[115] It struck me immediately that this early life history gave Russell something important in common with Hazel. Neither of them had been raised by their biological fathers, and both had been children of divorce in an era where such a thing would have been taboo.

At Yale, Russell had pursued a course of study in general science and then gone on to work with Firestone Tires, traveling to Argentina for work frequently throughout the 1930s and into the beginning of the next decade. His home base during those years had been Akron, Ohio, where he lived with his wife, a woman named Mary Frances Hughes Burke.[116] I noted the Akron years with some interest because during 1940, my father and Hazel had also lived in Akron while Dad took a course in statistics at the university there. I soon figured out they had lived a mere five minutes from each other, on intersecting streets. Even more intriguing, I discovered that Russell's mother, Genevieve Burke, lived literally around the corner from Dad and Hazel.

Russell might very well have been spending a great deal of time at his mother's house. His stepfather, Walter, has just died, and perhaps she was lonely. Maybe she was looking to sell her house and needed her son's help. It seems likely that Hazel met Russell all those years ago in Akron. And if Hazel had known Russell, then had my father too? If he hadn't, it certainly might indicate that Hazel and Russell had a romantic connection even then.

I managed to turn up a piece of information that indicated that, in all probability, my father had known Russell Burke. Amongst my father's papers, I discovered a very intriguing letter written to my father from a man named Martin Horrell of Horrell & Associates. Mr. Horrell begins by stating "McCann-Erickson has sent us your radio play *Acme Service* since we are the producers of the Grand Central Station program."[117]

Why would someone at McCann-Erickson feel compelled to send one of my father's plays to anyone? I suppose he might have sent it to them directly. Perhaps one of their clients was the sponsor for the show. But this seemed a little convoluted to me. I couldn't help wondering if Dad had used a contact at McCann to help him submit the radio play. Russell Burke worked at McCann at that time. Might my father have counted Russell Burke as a friend?

My father and Hazel lived in Akron for only eight months. My father gives no indication in anything he has written that their marriage was not a happy one at that time. But Hazel may have felt differently. It is clear that she felt torn between him and her mother, who clearly had no great affection for my father. The conflict that their disagreements caused Hazel might well have begun to chip away at the happiness that the couple seemed to have experienced in their early years together.

It could be that Hazel and Russell had lived so very close to one another during their early adult years but never met at all. I know that they knew each other a decade later while living in New York, but I could not be sure if this was the beginning of their acquaintance or a reunion of two people who knew each other very well.

The archivist at Yale had also told me something of Burke's career path, up until 1949 when he had stopped all communication with the Alumni Office. Apparently, after that time, repeated efforts had been made to contact him but without success.

Yale reported that he had worked for Firestone in four different cities, one of them being Akron, and this also led him to employment with Firestone's competitor, Goodyear.[118] Eventually, he had made his way to New York, and by the mid-1940s, he was a copywriter for the well-known advertising firm, McCann Erickson. He left McCann to work for Grant Advertising on 5th Avenue, a firm that was once a powerhouse in the ad world but which went out of business about a decade later.[119]

Yale also informed me that it would appear he and his wife had never had any children. This was bad news for me because following a line of offspring into the present day would seem to be the only way I could ever find a living being to talk to who knew anything about this man.

If Russell had not had children, I would have to look elsewhere for those living beings. And so I began to investigate his wife's family. Her name was Mary Frances Hughes, and with a bit of sleuthing, I uncovered the names of two brothers and a sister. Of the three siblings, only one yielded any possibilities. Her brother, Robert, had had two children, Anne and Thomas. A bit more sleuthing, and I located both of them: still living, one in Massachusetts and the other in Connecticut.

I had no email addresses for either of them, but thanks to dogged internet searching, I had possible snail mail locations. I wrote them both a letter, and included in the envelope a printout of a photograph of Russell Burke from the Yale yearbook, as well as a self-addressed stamped envelope, to make it very easy for them to respond.

A week went by and there was no response. And then, in my mailbox, I found my letter to Anne returned to me, with a scrawled message across the envelope that there was no forwarding address. I found another possible address to send it to. I mailed the letter again and continued to wait.

Another week passed, and I had all but given up any hope of a reply, when I spotted one of my self-addressed envelopes in my mailbox. I hurried inside the house and tore it open. It was from Thomas (Tom), the nephew of Russell Burke:

> I was quite surprised by your letter, since I haven't thought of my Aunt Frances for some time. I'll tell you what I know, but I'm afraid I don't have very much information to help you resolve your mystery.
>
> Frances was my father's […] oldest sister […] Although we lived just a few miles from Aunt Frances, I recall meeting her on only a couple of occasions. I have no recollection of having met Uncle Russell. I do recall when I was a kid—probably about 7 or 8—asking my parents why Aunt Frances' last name was "Burke," to which they informed me that it was her married name. I'm sure I asked, "Where is her husband?" only to learn that they were no longer together.
>
> On the few occasions the topic arose, my parents always spoke highly of Russell. My recollection is that they very much missed having him in their lives, limited as it likely was.[120]

Tom Hughes told me he was sorry he could not be of more use, but I quickly wrote him back that he had actually been very helpful. Now I knew that Russell's wife had gone by the name Frances, and not Mary, and more important, that she and Russell had likely split up around the mid-1940s, which was about the same time that Hazel and Dad had parted ways. I asked him a few more questions in a subsequent letter, included another self-addressed envelope, and crossed my fingers for additional information.

Tom Hughes didn't write me back, but he seemed to have passed the baton to his sister, Anne. One day I found an email from her in my inbox, and she and I began a regular correspondence. She provided me with a lot of information about her family but unfortunately, very little about Russell.

Ancestry sent me a surprising message one day. A fellow member had made an alteration to one of the census records I had saved for Burke. Who was this person who felt qualified to make corrections in the record for a man who was still to me mostly a mystery? I immediately sent him a query, wondering if I would hear anything back.

I did. It turned out that he was a distant relation to Burke and had been researching him just as I had. He shared with me his extensive family tree, which included associations and links for Russell that I had not known.

What I was slowly putting together for Russell Burke was not a fully-fleshed story of the man who had figured so significantly in Hazel's life. Instead, it was merely a resume. A dry biographical listing of where he had lived, the companies he had worked for. I could follow every step of his geographic and career path through his life, but the overall picture it produced was flat. I still had no idea how he had met Hazel or what exactly had transpired between them. I desperately needed an informant who had known him or at the very least knew someone who had heard his story.

I turned my attention to the Carr family. After Russell's father had divorced his mother, he had remarried. His second wife's name was Blanche, and with her he fathered two more sons, named Donald and Arthur. I was able to track down Arthur's granddaughter, Jackie Vaughan, who told me that Donald's daughter, Judith, was still alive. It seemed to me entirely probable that Russell might have sought out his biological family,

that Judith might have met her Uncle Russ. I would try everything I could think of to find Judith.

As I searched for people who had known him, I speculated
often about Russell's place in Hazel's life. Most of the information
I had pointed to him having been someone of great importance
to her. For one thing, he was the very first person mentioned in
the will, coming even before her father. And, of course, he had
been left a great deal of money. Moreover, she also left him some
other things of consequence, including her diamond ring. I had
to wonder if it was an engagement ring, and if indeed that ring
was from Russell. It wasn't something my father had given to her.
This was the very ring that had been stolen in Mexico, and when
questioned, my father did not know anything about it.

Hazel also left him something called an Ansley Dynaphone.
This was a record player, and a very good one. I recalled how in Dad's
book *The Distant Hill*, one of the things they had enjoyed doing
was listening to music together. And after all, Hazel was a singer. I
imagined she and Russell spending many evenings together listening to records, perhaps dancing alone in the apartment.

Hazel also left him all of her furniture, a bequest that seemed
an odd one to me unless the furniture meant something to him,
too. That fact made me wonder if they had been living together,
but given the era, it would be impossible to know for sure; 1950s
propriety would have surely dictated that their cohabitation, if it
happened, would have been covert.

Still, the biggest mystery of all for me remained: Why had she
made a will in the first place? She was only thirty-eight years
old! Why would she be willing away items she owned as a young
woman if she expected to live to be old? If she had expected to
live for a long time, the Dynaphone would be long outmoded,
and surely her furniture would have long since been traded out.

And if Russell was indeed her lover—and the amount of money
bequeathed to him certainly seems to imply that their relationship was still a significant one at the time of her death—why was

she on the cusp of moving away to Mexico, even as she knew that
he could be found far away, in Detroit? Russell did, in fact, have
a connection to the region: he served as the Latin-American
liaison both for Goodyear,[121] during his Akron days, and for
McCann-Erickson, while he was in New York,[122] but by the time
he made another move to Detroit, it's difficult to think that they
were still planning on being together.

So I had to wonder: had Hazel been planning to die the whole
time?

If Russell experienced any kind of devastation about the loss
of Hazel, I can find no proof of it. Because the will was snagged
for two years by legal challenges, Russell had to wait until 1953
to receive his money. By that time he had taken out a loan in
anticipation of the $10,000 and owed money to the Bank of
Detroit.[123] The tax file on her will had revealed to me that he
was already spending that money before he even received it.

I also learned that Russell had been engaged to marry just
four months after Hazel died. In late June, an announcement
appeared in the *Detroit Free Press* stating that he and a woman
named Catherine Wallace Martin would marry in October of
that year—1951.[124] Martin went by the name Kay and was a soci-
ety-page reporter for the *Free Press*. Surely Russell must have
courted Kay months before Hazel's death. Or had the courtship
been a whirlwind one? Either way, it was increasingly clear to
me that Russell Burke had not been inconsolable in the weeks
and months following Hazel's death.

I paid money to have a search done through Michigan's
state records. As I suspected from my newspaper searches, the
October wedding never took place. Kay Martin came from a
very wealthy family. Did the delay caused by the lengthy probate
of Hazel's will spoil Russell's plans? I already knew that he had
had to borrow money on the promise of his inheritance. Did Kay
grow tired of waiting? Or did he betray Kay as he may also have
betrayed Hazel? Kay Martin died a fairly young woman, in 1973,

just a few months before my father. According to the obituary I
found, she had never married.[125]

*   *   *

That summer that I was researching Russell Henderson Burke
proved to be the briefest of respites in my personal life. My sister's cancer appeared to be in remission, and she was scheduled
in July for reconstructive surgery. In fact, she came to stay at
my house with me the night before her surgery, and we talked
throughout the evening about my progress on the book, my theories about who Burke had been in Hazel's life, and about what
might have happened to destroy the relationship she had had
with our father.

Terri was as excited as I was about the discoveries I had made,
as I knew she would be.

No one else in this world could possibly have the deep and
personal interest in this quest that Terri and I shared. After losing Dad as early as we did in our lives, we had kept him alive
between us through our memories and our storytelling. But
until now, all we had had to work with were the recollections
of two young girls about a man we saw solely as "Daddy." Now
there were new facts coming to light, and the picture that we
had of our father was developing and changing with each new
discovery.

I filled her in on everything that I was learning, and it deep-
ened a bond between us that had always been there but had
grown more distant during the years we lived apart, raising our
own families. Now, as I added to our storehouse of information,
it was as though we were kids again, talking across the darkness
between our two beds long after we were supposed to be asleep.

That evening, after we had exhausted every theory and spec-
ulation we could, after we had regaled each other with many of
the old stories, I suggested to Terri that we take a stroll around

the neighborhood before going to bed. As we set off from my house, she turned to me and grabbed my hand, placing it just under her collarbone.

"Do you feel that?" she asked.

Beneath my fingertips, beneath her skin, there was a small, hard knot. I felt anxiety rise up in me but tried not to let it show on my face.

"Do you think it is anything to worry about?" she continued.

"I don't know," I said, "But when we get to the hospital tomorrow, you should definitely have your surgeon examine it."

When the surgeon felt the small lump, he elected to do only a partial reconstruction, in the event that implants might obstruct any tests that needed to be done. Later, her oncologist dismissed it as nothing more than scar tissue from her chemotherapy port.

But the oncologist was wrong.

Terri would live for only six more months. Her cancer had metastasized. The events that followed came at us so relentlessly that conversations about my book and our father were set aside, overwhelmed by developments of far greater consequence.

I would have to uncover the rest of the story alone. When Terri died, I lost my sister and my best friend. But I also lost the only other living survivor of the childhood we knew. If there was any hope that the story might live beyond me, I would need to be the one to tell it.

*   *   *

After a great deal of searching, I managed to acquire Russell Henderson Burke's death certificate. He had died of cancer and been cremated. At the end of his life, he lived in a humble garden-style apartment in Long Beach, apparently alone, for it seems that the only one available to speak for him, to provide information, was the neighbor living in the next apartment.[126] There was no second wife. No child. No one I could seek out to answer any of my questions. And his circumstances were far from luxurious. What had become of all the money that Hazel had left to him?

Had he retired to California, thinking to live out the rest of his life amid palm trees and sunshine? He had only lived there for two and a half years before cancer robbed him of the golden years he hoped for. He was sixty-eight years old. His last known employer was the George Reuter Organization in Chicago, factory of industrial films. His job title was copywriter.[127] I couldn't find anything more, at least not by looking at his employment history.

I turned to looking into Russell's stepfather's family, which led me to what I think is an enlightening discovery. For so long, I had hunted for Walter Burke but could find no evidence of him before his adult years. He had no childhood records and did not appear in a census prior to 1910.

The answer, when it came, was startling. It was because he had not begun his life as Walter Burke at all but rather as Walter Sanchez, son of Edward and Rose Burk Sanchez. Although Edward Sanchez had been born in Florida, his family had come originally from Mexico.[128]

This explained why Russell Burke was conversant enough in Spanish to serve as a liaison, and perhaps this also explained what had drawn Hazel to Mexico City. I couldn't help but wonder if there had been a plan that she would meet Russell there, one that might have fallen apart with their relationship, breaking her heart and leaving her alone in a foreign country, vulnerable to whatever loneliness and desolation plagued her.

Over the course of my investigation into Burke, I wrote to almost every living family connection I could find. This meant that I spoke with those who were only children when they knew him. It would seem he was not a man who interacted easily with children, leaving only the vaguest of recollections. Bruce Henderson, the son of Burke's first cousin, told me that "Cousin Russell" came each Thanksgiving and Christmas to visit his father and that he came bearing gifts—ones that Bruce surmised Burke's secretary must have selected for him. Bruce says he does not remember the sound of this cousin's voice, his face or his laugh, but rather, only that he seemed a traveler in a strange land, uneasy there among the young parents with their growing families.

It seems that each search I have begun has turned up only more questions. I could push on, keep asking questions, continue to hypothesize, but I could not prove anything. Facts were the only things that mattered. Finally, I realized that I would have to let my speculations go.

How sad it seems to slip from this world with nothing more to mark one's passing than a death certificate filed in a county courthouse. Though I have searched various newspapers to find out if he merited an obituary, I have come up with nothing. Why did his cousins not pay to have an obituary published in the Chicago paper? Did no one care that he was gone?

For weeks, I had been hoping that the death certificate would contain some clue that would crack the story wide open. Now I knew that I would have to concede that there was no more to be found. I would have to turn to a new avenue in my search to understand Hazel's final years: the annulment of her marriage to my father.

Pretend It Never Happened

The first two pages of Hazel's will file discussed in great detail Dad and Hazel's annulment. I knew that it had taken place in New York state. I knew the county. I knew the exact courthouse where it had been granted. And I was shocked to learn the grounds on which the annulment had been sought: Hazel charged my father with fraud and false representation.[129]

I knew little about this area of law, so I had no way of making even a guess as to what this might have meant. My father? Fraud? This did not seem to me even remotely possible. What could he have possibly done or claimed to merit this charge? My father had always been scrupulously honest and had insisted on the same from both my sister and me. I had to learn more.

In the course of my research, I have found many people willing and eager to give me whatever information they can provide about former family members, friends, and neighbors; I have also encountered countless dead ends and unwilling participants, those for whom the past was either too painful or entirely inaccessible. But I was about to encounter someone very different: a vigilant watchdog of New York state's divorce and annulment records.

Foolishly, I believed that it would be an easy matter to make a phone call and request a copy of that annulment. I wasn't prepared for the intractability of the New York laws. Nor was I prepared for a woman I will name here as Agnes. This is not her real name, but as everything I will recount here about her is both true and scathing, I feel it prudent to disguise her identity.

My call was directed to her line, and she answered in a strong and decidedly brusque New York accent. I assumed my most pleasant and polite self, instilled in me early in life by my Alabaman and oh-so-mannerly Mama: "Hello, my name is Melanie McCabe, and I have been doing some research into my father's life."

Agnes cut me off. "Well, isn't that nice for you?" Her tone was so snide and dismissive, I stumbled for a moment in my delivery.

"Yes," I continued. "And in my research, I have discovered that my father's first marriage was annulled, in your court, and so I am calling to ask how I might obtain—"

"That won't be possible."

I pushed on. "I want to request a copy of the annulment file."

She spoke rapidly, spitting out a speech that she had clearly made many times before. "All New York divorce and annulment records are sealed for a period of one hundred years. No one may break that seal until the hundred years have passed."

"The annulment occurred a very long time ago," I said. "In 1947. That's over sixty years ago."

"And so the files will be available then in 2047. A hundred years."

"But I am his daughter. I have proof of this, and can provide a copy of his death certificate…"

"That's very nice, but it doesn't make any difference. Now, if you like, I can provide for you a certificate verifying that the annulment took place, and it will be embossed with the seal of the state of New York."

"I don't need a certificate of verification. I already know that the annulment took place. What I need is the file about the case. The details of it."

"That file is sealed."

"And you're telling me that there is absolutely no way that I might be able to see that file?"

"Well," she said, her voice hard and sarcastic. "You could get a court order—but good luck with that."

"How does one get a court order?" I asked her.

"That's not my problem," she said. "Now is there anything else I can help you with today?"

"No," I said, defeated. "Not a thing."[130]

I had lost the battle, but I dug in my heels and decided to win the war. That evening I posted a question on Facebook: Does anyone know an attorney licensed to practice in New York state?

I was surprised to receive a message from a friend of mine from my MFA poetry days. I knew he was an attorney, as well as a poet. He told me he was licensed in New York and would be happy to help me. I thanked him profusely, and hastened to add that I would most certainly pay him. He wrote back, telling me what his standard per-hour billing rate was -- a staggering amount that made my stomach drop -- and added, "Don't worry. I'll present this to my firm as a possible pro bono case. Something we can take on to benefit the arts."[131]

As I waited for the painfully slow wheels of justice to turn, I thought a lot about the charges that Hazel had made in order to secure the annulment: fraud and false representation. My attorney had shared with me several legal articles about the history of annulment in New York, and it had been enlightening. I had learned that annulments were often chosen over divorces because, strangely enough, they were easier to obtain. At the time that Dad and Hazel split up, the only ground for divorce in New York was adultery. This resulted in New York state having an unusually large number of suits for annulment. Of the grounds provided by statute for annulment of marriage, fraud was by far the most commonly used. The fraudulent misrepresentation had to be of some material fact so that if it had not been practiced, the party who was deceived would never have consented to the marriage. One of these false claims might be the desire to have children; another might be as simple as falsely claiming to love the other person.

This new information called into question the idea that my father must have done something to betray Hazel; it may have been that fraud charges were trumped-up legal speak.

Still, I wondered about what she thought of his book, *The Distant Hill*. It was so clearly a thinly-veiled memoir of their marriage, and it painted a highly unflattering portrait of Hazel's mother, Florence, not to mention depicting Hazel as an alcoholic. If my father had shared it with her, his portrayal of events might have done little to soothe the probably rocky state of their marriage.

I considered the possibility that what caused strife in their marriage was the aftermath of Emma's death. As soon as Hazel learned that she had received very little in Emma's will, she prepared to do battle, enlisting the services of the Kramer family attorney, William W. Crowdus. I could well imagine that when she first received the news, she was a mixture of furious, afraid, and hysterical. Would my father have shared her reaction? I tried to imagine his response, based on the man I knew through my childhood. While I could believe that he might have been upset that she had been treated unfairly, I think he may well have counseled her to let it go, to not pursue legal action. It would, after all, cause an irreparable rift in the family, and it would consume a great deal of time and a considerable amount of the money she already had. Had they argued over this? Had they separated because of it? If so, it was all the more intriguing that Hazel had enlisted my grandparents to testify for her. Perhaps my father, feeling burned by the dissolution of their marriage, refused to do so. Or it could be something more innocent, that he felt himself incapable to testify, perhaps because of his deafness.

Or maybe it had come down to money, and nothing more. The Kramers had never thought much of my father as a choice for Hazel, and apparently they had not been all that keen on my grandparents either. I remembered the letter from Emma that I had found as a part of the court case in Chicago, where she wrote to her daughter, Hazel Bagby, not to let my grandparents ever get their hands on her money. In reference to Hazel McCabe, Emma wrote: "I only feel so sorry for you after we are dead and gone she will fight you tooth & toenail but you try & have an understanding with her instead of letting a Lawyer handel [sic] it—you get one-third & see that you get it not that those McCabes get it his Father & Mother are not so old but they can use it when we saved to accumulate it."[132]

Maybe it was Emma's adamant stand against the McCabes inheriting any of her money that motivated Hazel to seek the annulment. Perhaps she wanted to make sure that there was no impediment to her receiving a more equitable share of Emma's fortune. If Emma had not wanted Dad to get any of it, well, then. She would make sure he did not by having the marriage annulled.

These were the various theories I had considered for what drove Dad and Hazel apart. But of course, there was one more, involving the same story I first heard insinuated by my mother all those years ago, the one that seemed all but confirmed by the emergence of Russell Burke: Hazel and a lover.

I wondered also about the effect that pursuing this annulment must have had on my father. I believe he must have agreed to it, reluctantly, but I doubt he welcomed it. For one thing, he was the defendant in the case. He was the one being accused of something underhanded. I tried to imagine him telling all of this to his parents, the shame he must have felt. An annulment would be a declaration that the marriage had never existed. I believe that Dad loved Hazel deeply. And now, it would be as though the love they had shared had never happened at all.

My attorney started the ball rolling in an effort to obtain the annulment record, but the first step in that process involved dealing with Agnes. For more than half a year, she was uncooperative and rude in almost every interaction. At last, we went ahead and filed a petition for the record, even though we had no definite proof that it even still existed. The petition claimed that the charge of fraud against my father was causing me anxiety and stress because I did not know what the charge was founded on. And, in truth, this was not a fabrication. I *was* anxious and stressed. It had become incredibly important to me to learn what had ended this marriage.

I waited excitedly for the outcome. I knew that the odds were greatly against my being granted permission to see the annulment records, but I held onto a sliver of hope that things might work out, in spite of the odds.

Unfortunately, when the bad news came, it was even worse than I had expected.

The judge denied the petition, stating that the petitioner had "failed to demonstrate a sufficient basis to warrant overcoming the statutory protections pursuant to Domestic Relations Law Section 235." The secrets of my father's and Hazel's separation were denied to me. But worse, there was no hope for any kind of an appeal.

My attorney sent me an article that seemed to me almost like a twisted joke. On the first weekend in February 2015, in the Williamsburg section of Brooklyn, an enormous and still-raging fire had engulfed a warehouse on the waterfront. What had been stored in that warehouse? Extensive files from completed cases tried in Brooklyn, Queens, and Manhattan, and housed there by the New York state court system. Among these files were family court records such as divorces and annulments. The fire was still burning.[133]

"Do you think Agnes set it?" I asked my attorney, when I had recovered enough to make a feeble joke.

Perhaps it was a blessing my petition had been denied. Had I won, only to find that I would never see the records because they had been incinerated, I would have been devastated.

SOMETHING CLOUDY BECOMES CLEAR

Though he had written two full-length books, quite a number of short stories, and at least a dozen plays, literary success always eluded my father. Long before I was born, he had been actively writing and submitting his work. As I soon discovered going through files containing some of his old letters, Dad had a literary agent, and their letters indicate that he was doggedly persistent in his efforts to achieve literary fame.

When I was a girl, I fell asleep each night to the sound of him typing. The staccato clackety-clack of typewriter keys, the emphatic ding of the carriage return, was a familiar lullaby that my sister and I learned to sleep through, if we hoped to sleep at all. While he was writing *A Superior View*, his agent had expressed concern to him that the book would not have a wide enough audience to interest a publisher. My father's reaction was to immediately plan a family vacation to Superior so that he might make the rounds with everyone he knew in town who could be in a position to help him market such a book. For Terri and me, it proved a somewhat boring, chilly holiday, visiting Dad's old haunts and the school he had attended as a boy. We had only the vaguest idea then that this was more than a vacation for my father. It was a mission.

When my mother sold our family home in 1986, I raided the boxes that contained what was left of Dad's work. I lugged home with me that day a considerable trove of plays and stories. *The Distant Hill*'s more than five hundred pages were overflowing a warped and scuffed purple box, but it was *A Superior View* that was my heaviest prize. It was so long that it was bound in multiple volumes and seemed important by virtue of its heft alone.

Despite my father's unceasing efforts throughout my childhood, he achieved success only twice. And that success was far below what he desired. The only "book" he ever published was a pamphlet intended for children entitled *Animals That Give Milk*, which, incidentally, can still be purchased via Amazon. And if one looked at the listing for "milk" in the *Encyclopedia Americana* back in my childhood years, one would discover that the entry was written by my father. I can remember dragging friends of mine to this volume in the Arlington County Library. "See?" I'd tell them. "My father wrote this."

I discovered my father's play, *Waverly Place*, in a late-night frenzy of googling. I was surprised to find it listed on Google Books, but not shocked that it actually existed. The title seemed familiar to me. I thought it very likely that I had once found it among my father's many plays.

But I no longer possessed it, if I ever had. And if I had once held it in my hands, it had been when I was much younger and far more ignorant about Dad's former life. I saw that it was part of a collection at the New York Public Library. Why was it there? Had it ever been produced? Why this particular play and none of the others?

I emailed the library and was directed to someone in their archive department. She had no knowledge of the provenance of the manuscript, but yes, I could obtain a copy of the play if I sent a copy of Dad's death certificate, to indicate both that he was deceased and my relationship to him. And I would also need to pay them $100.

I wrote back, "So I have to pay for my own father's play?"

Unfortunately, the answer was yes. It seemed to me like a lot of money for what amounted to photocopying, and I had no idea whether the play was in any way related to my Dad and Hazel. In fact, it was very likely that it was not. I had many plays he had written, and none seemed to be about his own life. But the thought of it, sitting in some dusty vault in Manhattan, perhaps containing some valuable piece of information I did not know, tormented me, and so I sent the money.

It turned out to be one of the best investments I had made in my search thus far.

The play was scanned and a disk sent to me. As soon as I looked at the cast of characters, I knew I had something valuable. The main characters were named Lydia Eldridge and Barney Eldridge, the same names Dad had used as pseudonyms for himself and Hazel when he wrote the short story, "A New Look For Lydia." And as I began to read, I realized with a thrill of excitement that he was writing about their marriage, about the period of time after World War II when he had returned home to her and Manhattan. The opening statement about the setting reads, "The entire play takes place in Lydia Eldridge's apartment in Greenwich Village, New York City. It is Spring, 1946."[134]

As I clicked to each new image, I became increasingly certain that by the time I finished the play, I would have answers to many of the questions that had plagued me throughout my long search. Early in the first scene, the main character, Lydia, receives a phone call from her husband, Barney, who is unexpectedly home from overseas. Another woman named Hilary is with her in her apartment when Barney calls. She appears to be Lydia's good friend and helps her to prepare for Barney's arrival as Lydia becomes increasingly anxious and high-strung. At one point, Hilary seems to imply that Barney's showing up with no warning is an attempt to take Lydia off-guard, to "catch" her unaware.

What was this about, I wondered. What had Lydia been doing that she wouldn't want Barney to know about? I grew even more excited. Surely, this must have something to do with another man. Perhaps I was about to find out at long last about the mysterious Russell Henderson Burke. I read on, eager to get to the end. What waited for me in the ensuing pages was something I had never expected in any of my many wild-theory surmises.

If through this play my father was indeed providing a barely-fictionalized glimpse into his first marriage, then it would appear that it was not Hazel's involvement with another man that had been the problem at all. It was her involvement with another woman. In the last scene of the play, Barney Eldridge leaves Lydia because of her relationship with her close friend and neighbor, Hilary. It is never expressly stated that it is a romantic or sexual relationship, but it is heavily implied throughout the whole drama.

Near the beginning of the play, Hilary shows jealousy when Lydia puts Barney's photograph on the bureau; later, she hides it in a drawer and replaces it with a photograph of herself. Throughout the opening scenes, Hillary hovers near Lydia, touching her, kissing her on the cheek. She is demanding of Lydia's time and seems threatened and jealous of Barney's presence.

Near the end of the play, Lydia pleads with Barney not to leave her when he realizes that she has been involved with Hilary.

BARNEY: You lived a lie–every day since I've been back. Yes, even while I was gone. Your letters—lies.

LYDIA: They weren't. I meant them.

BARNEY: I'm supposed to believe that?

LYDIA: Yes, I did mean them. Oh, if you only knew…

BARNEY: Yet you lied when I came back. How do I know you're not still lying?

LYDIA: I'm not. Oh, I couldn't tell you. I couldn't. I was ashamed to tell you. And she wouldn't let me go! She threatened me. She said she would tell you... I hate her and all that she did to me—to us. But what about you? How can you ever... Oh, what do you think of me? You hate me, I know.

BARNEY: No, I don't hate you.

LYDIA: Oh, if you had only come back sooner.

BARNEY: It would have been the same.

LYDIA: No, no. If you hadn't had to go away when you did.

BARNEY: You had already fallen in with Hilary.

After I told Chris about it, and he had read the play himself, he said, "Well, there may be no truth in this at all. It might be entirely fictionalized. How can you possibly know?"

I considered this for a moment, then shook my head. "I don't think this is something that would have ever occurred to my father to invent."

The play was written in 1948, and the inclusion of a lesbian relationship in the plot would surely have marginalized its marketability. And my father was avidly seeking publication. Why would he have made up a development like this that would have kept many theatrical companies from going anywhere near *Waverly Place*?

Still, I mulled over Chris's question and was struck by something I had never known as fully as I did at that moment: how very little I really knew of my father. What he had revealed to me when I was a child, an adolescent, was only one side of who he was. To me, he was Daddy. A loving father. Inveterate prankster. Tireless storyteller. But I certainly knew nothing of him as a man outside of our home on Vernon Street, the person he presented to the adult world when there were no daughters close at hand to observe him.

What did my father know about homosexuality? What did he think about gay men? About lesbians? In my experience of him, he had always been extremely liberal in his politics and was an avid supporter of the civil rights movement. Did this openness to bucking established norms carry over into his views on homosexuality? Or, on this matter, was he very much a product of his time?

I have only one memory of my father that is in any way connected to his views on gays, and it is not a flattering one. Just a week or so before he went into the hospital, I had invited a boy I liked over to the house and introduced him to Dad. This boy was slight, small-boned, shy and awkward. Dad gave him one of his booming "hellos" and shook my friend's hand. Later, when the boy turned away and could not see my father, Dad looked at me pointedly, shaking his head as though to imply that I had made a very unwise choice, and then made the stereotypical limp-wristed gesture that made clear he thought my friend something less than manly.

This one incident provides only the smallest bit of anecdotal evidence. I had no idea at all what my father thought of lesbianism. The general thinking at that time, of course, was that homosexuality was an illness, one that needed to be cured rather than accepted. The way that Lydia's relationship with Hilary is portrayed gives every indication that Dad may have bought into this belief. A character in the play named Jean, after meeting Hilary, shares the following with Barney: "I've seen women like Hilary before. There were some in the WAC;

we even had some in the Nurses' Corps...The women I am talking about aren't even women. They are something different—indescribable." Jean warns Barney to get Lydia away from Hilary because Lydia is weak.

I have a great deal of trouble believing that my father would have voluntarily made this lesbian relationship a part of his play if it were not true. Or, at least, very close to the truth. It just didn't seem to me be the sort of thing that would have occurred to him, or a subject that he would have dreamed of exploring unless it had in some way entered his real life.

There was, in *Waverly Place,* some room for nuance. In Dad's depiction of this relationship between Lydia and Hilary, the overriding reason he seems to be suggesting for Lydia's involvement with Hilary is that she is a weak person who is easily led by stronger, manipulative personalities. Throughout the play, much is made of Hilary being similar to Lydia's mother, who controlled her and made her a nervous wreck. As I had already discovered through *The Distant Hill*, court testimony and Leverich's book on Williams, Florence Kramer was exactly this sort of dominating and possessive personality.

Was Dad suggesting that Lydia's involvement with Hilary was not because of her sexual inclinations, but rather, because she was a submissive personality who was looking to replicate the unhealthy relationship she had had with her mother? If this was so, then Lydia (or Hazel) might have become involved with either male or female who took on a dominating role with her.

This theory seemed to work better when also trying to deal with the presence of Russell Henderson Burke in her life.

It now seemed more likely to me that Burke became a significant factor in Hazel's life after she had split up with my father. No mention is made in *Waverly Place* of any man who might represent Burke. If I take a leap of faith and use the play as a sort of blueprint for the truth, then it would seem Russell became someone of great

importance to Hazel after the summer of 1946. The annulment
was granted in December 1947. She was also thoroughly preoc-
cupied through that year by her grandmother's death in April and
the ensuing challenge to her grandmother's will. Although I had
absolutely no reason for my supposition, I imagined that she and
Russell became involved some time in 1948.

But if she was involved in a lesbian affair, how did this occur?
What happened that ended things with the woman my father
called Hilary? The last page of *Waverly Place* suggests that Hazel
moved on from Hilary to another woman, "Marga." Was all of
this true? Was any of it true? I had thought I was dealing with a
straightforward case of infidelity and parting, but now nothing
made sense. One story seemed to contradict the other.

I had no idea how I would figure any of this out. But at least
now I knew that there was even more to discover than I had originally thought. And I was determined to do whatever I possibly
could to get to the truth.

*   *   *

I sensed that Tennessee Williams, one of the people who perhaps could understand Hazel best, might have been aware of
Hazel's sexual orientation. An observation from Williams in
the 1973 *Playboy* interview suddenly took on new meaning:
"My great female love was a girl named Hazel from St. Louis.
But she was frigid. She'd make me count to ten before she'd
let me kiss her; we were both 11 when we met and we were
sweethearts until she was in college. She said, 'Tom, we're
much too young to think about these things.' But I constantly
thought about sex."[135] Williams does not, of course, indicate
that Hazel's lack of interest in him has anything to do with her
possible interest in women, and even if Hazel were interested
in women, she still might have had interest in men. But I wondered what other insights his work might provide me.

I had read that Williams had written a play very late in his life called *Something Cloudy, Something Clear.* By his own admission, it was the most autobiographical of any of his plays, and in it, people from his life appear, actually bearing their own names. Most interesting of all to me was that Hazel appeared as herself and talked with the Williams character.

I mentioned the play to Chris, and he told me he would bring it with him from the library when he came to visit me that weekend. When I got my hands on the small volume, I quickly skimmed through it for Hazel's name. What I found was only mildly interesting. In it, a character named August is visited by apparitions from his past. A woman named Hazel appears, and they have a brief conversation about the relationship they had had when they were young. Nothing I hadn't already known. I shelved the book with my other books about Williams and turned my research in another direction.

That might have been the end of it. But one very lucky night, I was reading a book of criticism about Williams' plays when I came across a quotation from *Something Cloudy* that stopped me cold. The character August says that Hazel married a man named McCabe![136] How could that be? I had been all through that play and had not seen anything about Dad.

Looking back at the citation from the book of criticism, I saw that the line came from a typescript. This must have been an early version of the play. For some reason, in the final version, Williams had cut the mention of my father. What else had he cut? I needed to get a copy of that early version, and once more, Chris stepped in and saved the day. He found a copy of the script at Ohio State University and contacted a librarian there. When I spoke with him, he told me that he could not send me the whole play, but he would be happy to copy and send the few pages that mentioned Hazel and my father.

What I read there was far beyond my expectations, and raised for me a possibility that I had not even considered.

One evening, the main character, (named August in the script, but referred to at times as Tom—even written in at times, by hand, as "Tom"), encounters what is seemingly a female apparition in a surreal scene on a beach. In the stage directions, the girl is described as tall, with red-gold hair, and is identified as "a girl who was Hazel."

Hazel calls to him, using the name "Tom," the name she knew him by when they were young. Someone (Williams himself, I imagine) has scratched through "Tom" in the typescript I have and written in "August" instead.

August averts his face, and cries out, "No, no, not now! It's too late, not now"—meaning that the chance he and Hazel had to be together had long past, years ago. And perhaps could never have been because of Williams' homosexuality.

Hazel responds to the implied reference to his sexuality by saying, "I knew, you could have told, and I could have told you it didn't matter.—Tom?—I loved girls."[137]

My eyes widened as I read this. Was that really an underline under the word "I"? Yes—and in thick black ink. Was Hazel really saying what I thought she was saying? Was this the corroboration I had been looking for?

I continued reading. August goes on to tell her it made no difference, that all that mattered was that she *did* love. And he brings up a guilty secret that Hazel tells him she already knew about: that he had made a hole in a cubicle at the local pool to watch boys in the showers.

He reminds her that she once told him she would never hurt or embarrass him, and she replies by asking him if she ever had.

He answers, "No, but you married Terry McCabe."

She dismisses this statement with an offhand, "Oh, that."

When August responds, he seems to support my father. "He was a nice guy. Full of wild Irish humor. He loved you."

And then Hazel says something that hurt my heart, for I knew how the statement would have broken my father's. She replies:

"Yes, but the love part only lasted six months, the rest was—only loyalty. I told you that."[138] And then she drifts away from him.

Only six months! And whose love was it that had lasted so short a time? Although the way the exchange is constructed, Hazel might be saying that my father's love had only lasted for half a year, I knew in my core that this could not be true. I had read too much—of his plays, stories, and even his short autobiography—to put any stock in this idea. It was so painfully clear to me that he had loved her deeply, and for a long time. So the Hazel character must mean that it was she who had ceased to love my father.

But how and when was it that she had come to confess this to Tom Williams? "I told you that," she says. As I read on, I began to get a good sense of when that revelation might have taken place.

After Hazel departs, August returns to "real life," signaled by a change in lighting, and he resumes speaking with a character named Clare—the sister of a man named Kip, who was a former lover of Tennessee Williams'.

He asks Clare, "Has she gone?" but Clare does not know who he is talking about. He tells her, "The sweetest and kindest, perhaps the one most loved—had sense, had intuition enough to know that I would become what I am."

He then goes on to say something that startled me in all that it implied: "She went on liquor and pills, the same as I did later, and it killed her in Mexico City, that and the altitude and […] the guilt that made me fail her when she returned for understanding between us, a time when she was alone and I was with Frank."[139]

There is a lot packed into these few lines.

I already knew from reading the *Playboy* interview with Williams back in 1973 that he knew about Hazel's death, as well as my father's. But here, much more explicitly, he reveals that he knew precisely where and how she died. I was intrigued by his statement about the altitude in Mexico City. A bit of research revealed to me that the effects of alcohol could indeed be more potent at higher elevations. Hazel was a long-term heavy abuser of both alcohol and barbiturates. Had she been unaware that what she could tolerate back home in Manhattan might be enough to kill her in this city 7,200 feet above sea level? Had her death not been deliberate at all—but an accidental overdose?

Parsing out that sentence, it would seem that Williams attributed Hazel's death to substance abuse in an unfamiliar setting and to his own guilt about his sexuality, which led to his failure to help her when she needed it. The question for me was this: exactly when was this time of which he spoke? This time when Hazel returned to him for understanding, and he failed her? Figuring this out would help me confirm what I already suspected: that Hazel had continued to have contact with her good friend Tom long after other biographers thought their relationship was over.

My first instinct was to assume that it occurred in late May or very early June of 1947. It was on May 18, 1947, that Hazel had written to Tom, asking for his help in the court case she was bringing to overturn Emma's will. She wanted him to supply her attorney with his memories of the young Hazel's life with her grandparents. At the conclusion of the letter, she had suggested that he telephone her so that they might talk about their memories of those days. Had he done so? It seems likely to me, as within a week he had written to William Crowdus, Hazel's lawyer, with his recollections of those years.

It seems very likely to me, as well, that their phone conversation might well have led to a visit. Two old friends, sharing reminiscences, probably drinking heavily, and with that, a loosening of inhibitions that might have prompted Hazel to confess to Tom about her marriage to my father, and perhaps about her preference for women. My bet is that this meeting did take place, but I believe, also, that there was probably at least one subsequent meeting. And this is because of the remark that August makes about Frank in *Something Cloudy, Something Clear*.

Frank Merlo was Williams' long-term partner for well over a decade. They met in the spring of 1947, just about a month before Hazel sent Tom her letter asking for help. At that time, Williams was involved in an intense relationship with a highly volatile and temperamental man named Pancho Rodriguez, who was constantly causing scenes, getting into fights, and earning the distrust and distaste of many of Williams' friends and business associates. The evening Tom met Frank, there was a mutual attraction, and the two men slipped off to have a one-night-stand on the nearby Provincetown beach. That night, Pancho learned of the betrayal and went on a jealous rampage. Although Tom was quite taken with Frank, he did not see him again until about a year later, in the spring of 1948. At that point, their relationship took off.[140]

And so, since August says that Hazel sought him out for understanding when she was alone, and he was with Frank, it seems to me that this specific meeting could not have taken place in 1947. It had to have occurred at some point between 1948 and 1950. My bet is on 1948, as at some point after this encounter when Williams describes Hazel as being alone, it seems very likely that she may have acquired a lover. A male lover named Russell Henderson Burke.

Was Burke the only one in her heart? He merited the largest bequest from her will. But it seems highly probable that there was a woman—or women—who held a significant place, as well. The idea that Hazel might have had relationships with women, suggested in my father's play, was corroborated by Tennessee Williams. Why would these two men, so different in so many ways, both think to write about their Hazel stand-ins having homosexual love affairs?

If I wanted to get an outsider's view of Hazel's relationships, it seemed like there was only one other avenue open to me. I needed to take a deeper look at the people to whom Hazel had left her money.

THE MYSTERY WOMEN

I have no verifiable facts that Hazel was lesbian or bisexual. I have only intriguing hints and information that, when looked at, all of a piece, lead me to believe that it may well have been so. I can do no more here than discuss what I do know, and concede that time and bad luck and the maddening propensity people seem to have for throwing out old correspondence may have forever robbed me of knowing the truth.

In order to discover what I have been able to discover, I have had to hunt, stalk, and pursue relentlessly. I have searched on Google, Ancestry, Facebook, ProQuest, and I have journeyed to the Library of Congress to dig even deeper. As someone who is by nature fairly shy and retiring, this quest has forced me into behavior that I have found uncomfortable—and surprising.

I can make no definitive statement about the thoughts, secrets, and dreams of any of these women. All of them are now dead, and I have no correspondence or diaries that would enable me to see beyond surface facts. I have no proof of anything. I can only report what I do know and pose here the questions that I have tried for so long to answer.

ELEANOR KANDARIAN

On a warm late spring day in 1945, Eleanor and Hazel stretched languidly out on the thick white terry towels they draped over their deck chairs at the opulent hotel and spa in Tarrytown, NY. Waiters hovered nearby to offer drinks. My father was far away, in Cairo or Athens or Rome, fulfilling his service with the United Nations Relief and Rehabilitation Administration to aid war-torn Europe and North Africa. Did Hazel miss him at all? Eleanor, no doubt, had been filling Hazel's ears with her own dissatisfactions with married life. She wanted to make a break with her husband, Albert, but didn't yet know how to make it happen.

I had searched long and hard for this friend of Hazel's, and chased down a number of leads before finally locating her daughter, Eleanor (Ellie) Keane, who was one of the most helpful interviewees I spoke with. As a young girl, Ellie often accompanied her mother when she spent time with friends, and one of her mom's most frequent companions was Hazel. The two of them both had money to spend and seemed to enjoy many social activities with that money.

Eleanor was married to a man named Albert Kandarian, who owned and operated a restaurant in Rhode Island called The Chicken Roost. He had "made his first million by 1945," and Eleanor enjoyed all the many social activities this wealth afforded her. Ellie recalls spending time with her mother and Hazel at a very posh hotel/health spa in Tarrytown, New York. "It looked like a castle," she said, "and all the women wore white bathrobes."[141] It was in Tarrytown that Hazel taught Ellie to play canasta. She still marvels at the kindness and patience Hazel showed to a very young girl.

There were other trips: to Providence and to the beach near Pawtucket, Rhode Island. It was to the beach that Hazel appeared with a good-looking man at her side. Ellie remembered his name as "Roger," but I wondered if he might possibly have been

Russell Burke. I sent her a picture of Burke. She told me that he "looks like what I remember. The same dark hair. Black hair." It was a tantalizing possibility but far from certain.

Ellie told me that, in all, there must have been about eight to ten different occasions when she remembers spending time with Hazel. Eleanor was very likely one of her only affluent friends. Many of the others seemed to scrape by on clerical jobs, but with Eleanor, Hazel had someone with whom to indulge in luxuries that her other friends could not afford.

Upon hearing how well-off her family had been, I said to Ellie, "Well, I guess my theory must be wrong. When I learned that your parents had divorced shortly after Hazel died, I figured that the money Hazel left to your mom was what enabled her to make the break with your father, but it sounds as though that would not have been an issue for her."

"Oh, no," Ellie hastened to tell me. "Hazel's money is probably what made it possible. My father was giving her only $25 a week in alimony, and she left with just the clothes on her back."

I confided to Ellie Keane that I thought there was a strong possibility that Hazel had been either lesbian or bisexual. I did not make any further comment, but she quickly told me that her mother had not been, telling me about her second marriage to a man named Julius.

Although Hazel's generous bequest proved a godsend for Eleanor, Ellie told me that her mother had been shocked and shaken by Hazel's death. There had been no indication, as far as she was concerned, of depression or suicidal tendencies in her friend.

Her daughter would always remember her. Hazel was "stunning. Classy. Outgoing—and as big as life."[142]

ELIZABETH DOSSER

In a small café in Greenwich Village, Hazel sat with Eleanor Kandarian. Usually when she got together with Eleanor, it was just the two of them. Or, rather, the three of them, as Eleanor often brought along Ellie. But this afternoon, Hazel had invited another friend as well. A woman named Betty, who, according to Ellie, seemed nothing like her mother or Hazel. Betty wasn't dressed "to the nines," as were her two companions. She did not take pains with her appearance and was described as "rangy" and a bit odd.

"She was a Village Girl. A real Bohemian," Ms. Keane told me. "She sat herself by the window and kept her eye on all the people going by. She was studying people. If she found someone interesting, she put them into one of her stories."[143] Betty had told the little girl that she wrote and sold fiction for the "love magazines," romantic potboilers with steamy plots that sold well enough to augment her earnings in the library of the New York Times. When Ellie told me this, I thought about how Dad's play, Waverly Place, took place in Greenwich Village. I wondered if Betty had been a model for one of the characters in that play.

Ellie may not have believed her mother had any attraction toward women, but when we discussed Betty, she wasn't ruling anything out. "That would not surprise me," she told me.

Ellie identified a woman in a photo I sent her as the Betty she remembered from that day in Greenwich Village. The photo came from a series in the album I had of Hazel and a friend taking photos of each other one sunny day in Central Park. I had thought at first that the photo might have been of Ms. Keane's mother, Eleanor Kandarian, but she assured me it was Betty. And I realized that Betty almost certainly must have been Hazel's closest friend, Elizabeth Dosser. I compared it to the photo I had of her from her high school yearbook. About twenty-five years had passed between the photos, but the facial structure and features matched. I had finally found her.

Not counting her half-sister, the very first of the women to be mentioned in Hazel's will was Elizabeth Dosser. Because she was mentioned first, and because Hazel left her not only money, but an expensive bracelet and half of all of her wardrobe, I decided that Elizabeth must have been closer to her than anyone else. I had set out to learn as much about her as I possibly could.

Elizabeth was born in Tennessee on November 28, 1904, and on that same day, her mother, Estella Muir Dosser, died in childbirth.[144] What must a loss like that do to a person? To know that it was the very act of your being born that caused your mother to die. To never know your own mother except through photographs and other people's memories. To realize that your father might very well resent you because you are the reason he lost his wife. I considered how this emptiness, this lack of a parent, might well have formed a bond between Elizabeth and Hazel, a common background that might have helped to accelerate the deepening of their friendship.

Not long after this date, her father remarried, and soon thereafter, Elizabeth acquired a half-sister, Amanda. Elizabeth attended Knoxville High School and graduated in 1922. She is pictured in the yearbook alongside the caption, "Unassuming and sweet, she bloomed among us like a flower." She has a pleasant, though not pretty, face and a shy smile. She must have studied journalism as an undergrad—or else have been enormously talented and enterprising—because she worked as a reporter for the *Knoxville Sentinel* and then the *St. Petersburg Times* in Florida. A Tampa city directory lists her as an assistant publicity director in 1927-1928. She was clearly very ambitious, and by 1930, she had reached "the big time" of New York City. By the early 1930s, she was in attendance at Columbia University, presumably to get a graduate degree in library science, as subsequent census information lists her as a librarian, working in the Information Bureau of the *New York Times*. She also wrote some book reviews for the paper. She remained in New York, living in Greenwich Village, from 1930 until after Hazel died.[145]

No letter remains to tell me how they met. No family member or friend exists who knows the tale. But clearly, Elizabeth was dear to Hazel. The bracelet she left to her was valuable, not only monetarily, but sentimentally. She always wore it. And she had wanted it to belong to Elizabeth, perhaps as a constant reminder of their bond.

By 1954, at the age of fifty, Elizabeth was living in South Carolina in an apartment with her father, J. Harry Dosser, and listed in a city directory as employed as a freelancer. Her half-sister Amanda and Amanda's husband Frank Sells, a fundamentalist preacher, were also living in the same town and both taught at Columbia Bible College.[146] (The Reverend Sells, interestingly, was a noted speaker who claimed that Fundamentalism was under great attack from Satan.)

Elizabeth was ultimately paid a small sum in compensation for the bracelet she never received, the one that had been stolen in Mexico City. I like to think that the money meant far less to her than the bracelet would have. She died in 1975 at the age of seventy, unmarried and childless. And because there were no children, I had nowhere to go with my questions. Her sister Amanda also appears to have been childless. My queries to the Sells family and the Godmans (her mother's family) went nowhere.

If Elizabeth had had committed relationships with women, they would not have been traceable through any of the usual means. She would not have gotten a marriage license, for example, to publicly affirm any relationship she might have had. I am left only with questions, and some suspicions, about the nature of the relationship between Hazel and Elizabeth.

ROMAYNE LUTTER

The woman with whom Elizabeth would have to divide Hazel's clothes was named Romayne Lutter. As soon as I saw the name in the will, I felt a thrill of recognition and excitement. For so long, I had looked at that restaurant photo and thought that it said Romagne, and that this must indicate that it had been taken in France. But now I realized there was a good chance that the mystery woman in the photo was actually Hazel's friend, Romayne. She had lived in Milwaukee at the same time that Dad and Hazel had, and had taught piano. It seemed a good bet that she might have met Hazel through this music connection. Hazel must have stayed in touch with her through the years.

It was not lost on me that Romayne Lutter taught piano, just as did the character of Hilary in Dad's play, *Waverly Place*. Was Romayne the model for this character? Had she and Hazel had a relationship that extended beyond friendship, as Hilary and Lydia's seemed to? There are other indications that my father might have been suspicious of their relationship: in *The Distant Hill*, it is the character of Helen that the "Hazel character" Lizbeth runs to when her mother dies; Helen is the piano-playing accompanist that backs up Lizbeth when she sings. In both works, it is a woman who plays piano who causes strife and distance between the married pair.

Romayne lived to the astonishing age of 105 and married twice, but unfortunately, she had no children. And she had been an only child, so there were no sibling's children for me to pursue. I had only the photograph and an obituary that ran in a newspaper in Port Washington, Wisconsin.[147]

A little googling, however, turned up for me the name of a woman named Francine Barclay, a former student of Romayne's, still living in Port Washington and now a teacher herself. She and I spoke for over an hour, and she shared with me many insights about Romayne that gave me a lot to think about.

Francine began studying piano with Romayne when she was just five years old. As a child she perceived her as a caring and exacting teacher. After about nine years, however, Romayne felt that it was time for Francine to move on. She had reached an advanced level and needed a different teacher. Though Francine did indeed change teachers, she kept up a close friendship with Romayne all her life and gave the eulogy at Romayne's funeral.

Francine remembers her as a complex individual. She was youthful in her thinking, open-minded, and able to form friendships with people of all ages. She was very active, had many social engagements, and was an avid patron of the arts. But as she got older, she struggled more with various health issues, and there was "less joy in her life."[148] Francine shared with me that she thought it possible that Romayne was clinically depressed. Romayne let Francine know that she had had a lot of heartbreak in her life, and there was often an undertone of despair in her, something unspoken but felt.

Romayne had married Austin Lutter some time before 1930. But by 1940, they had divorced, and she was living alone.[149] Another informant from Wisconsin, whose mother had been close friends with Romayne, told me that the breakup of that marriage and Austin's swift remarriage were very hurtful to Romayne.[150] It would not be until 1959 that Romayne would remarry. She lived alone as a single woman for almost twenty years.

I shared with Francine my surmise that Romayne may have been the model for the characters of Hilary and Helen in my father's play and novel. I brought up the idea very tentatively, uncertain how she might react to such an insinuation, but she did not seem to take any offense or exception to this hypothesis at all.

"Who knows?" said Francine. "It wouldn't surprise me. She was willing to go out there and be experimental." She went on to tell me that Romayne had been friends with Liberace and had recommended that Francine continue her piano study with a man who was openly gay. "She had no problems with bisexuality or homosexuality."[151] She even added that Romayne, in the 1970s, already an elderly woman, had expressed an interest in trying marijuana.

I had mailed Francine the group photo that had so mystified me, and she confirmed that the woman on the right was Romayne. She also identified as Romayne another woman I had been uncertain about. In this photo, Hazel and Romayne sit astride mules in what appears to be a western and mountainous setting.

Her identification of Romayne in these two photos helped me to construct what happened in those mysterious months following Hazel's mother's death. From what my father had written in *The Distant Hill*, Hazel had fled Des Moines to return to Milwaukee, to visit the woman that Dad named Helen, a pianist. Florence had died at the end of May 1943. The group photo in the restaurant is dated June 27, 1943.

Hazel fled, and Dad pursued her. There they all are together. The caption continued to bewilder me. "My 11th post-operative day and I feel like a million." Somehow, the broken and grieving Hazel appears, just a month after her mother's death, beaming and out on the town. According to this caption, she had some sort of operation on June 16, 1943, just 18 days after Florence died. I discussed the strangeness of this with Francine.

"Maybe an abortion?" she suggested. I considered that, but thought it unlikely that Hazel would be blithely declaring this in writing on her photo.

"Possibly a miscarriage," I said.

But neither of us could know. No medical records are obtainable. No letters seem to exist.[152]

In Hazel's album, I found a train ticket stub from a trip she took to Colorado in August that same year. Colorado, I felt certain, was where the mule picture had been taken. Romayne had accompanied her on this vacation; my father had not gone along. Whether this was because of work obligations, or because he was not invited, I cannot say.

Who was Romayne to Hazel? Simply a good friend, or something more? Though I have searched hard for the answer to this question, I can prove nothing.

GWYN FERRIS

It seems strange to me, of all the women I have researched from
Hazel's will, that the one I have had the most trouble coming to
know is Gwyn Ferris. She certainly appeared the most frequently
in searches of the *New York Times* archive. Mentions of her were
also easy to come by at the archives of the *Atlanta Constitution*.
She was a multi-talented woman and achieved some acclaim as a
painter, a dancer, and an actress. I have found numerous notices
for various gallery showings of her art, as well as notices for her
dance and dramatic performances. But all that these notices provide me with are the bare facts of what happened. The where, the
when. Aside from a mention or two in which her paintings are
favorably commented upon, I have found nothing that tells me
anything about Gwyn the artist, the performer, or the woman.

She was born in Tennessee in 1906 and moved with her family
to Georgia shortly thereafter. She lived in Atlanta and as a very
young woman, acted in plays there,[153] and had paintings shown
at the Atlanta High Museum of Art.[154] She was clearly ambitious,
and it wasn't long before she had broken free of Atlanta and
moved to New York. There she met with more successes, in both
art and dance. I saw that a photo of her had appeared in *Dance
Magazine* in 1949 and eagerly sought a copy of it.[155] At least I
would know what she looked like! But when it arrived, I was
disappointed. Part of a group of dancers at a party, she is shown
in shadow, only her profile, and I could just make out enough to
see that she was blonde, pretty, and wearing what appeared to be
a leopard-fur hat.

Did Hazel attend one of her performances? Or a gallery
opening? Did they meet through a mutual friend? I wondered
whether Gwyn and Elizabeth knew one another from their days
in Tennessee.

I was intrigued that Gwyn was a painter. It was hard not
to think immediately of the character of Marga in Dad's play,

Waverly Place. Marga is also a painter and is clearly depicted as a lesbian with a lover named Betsy. Was this coincidence? Perhaps. But considering my father's propensity for basing his fictional works on his actual life, it seemed entirely possible that Gwyn could be the model for the character of Marga. It appears that Gwyn never married.

After much searching, I eventually tracked down a nephew of hers in Atlanta who seemed to know less about her than I did. He said she had visited them once when he was a child and knew that she was an artist. But he didn't remember her, never saw her again, and had no idea at all what became of Aunt Gwyn.[156]

MARIANNA JESSEN

I have no idea how Hazel came to know Marianna Jessen. Even after tracking down two of her nieces, and interviewing one of them, I still cannot figure out how they might have met. Marianna and her husband divorced some time shortly before or during World War II, and ever after, she lived as a single woman in New York, working in the oversight of kindergarten and day-care programs. Given that Dad and Hazel had no children, it isn't at all clear what would have brought them together.

As her niece, Mia, describes her, "she was a smart and competent woman, trapped, as so many good women of her generation were, in the old stereotype that a woman should be married with children. To be single, much less divorced, was a stigma." How well Hazel understood that truth. Having grown up herself with a divorced mother, Hazel must have known what that sort of judgment felt like. Perhaps having experienced it firsthand is what motivated Hazel to seek an annulment instead of a divorce.

I believe Hazel had an affinity for those who had been judged or ostracized in some way. Perhaps this is what drew her to Marianna. Her niece told me that Marianna "was a very private person. She did not talk about herself very much. I know, from the little she said, that she said that she felt overshadowed by her sister, my mother, who was outgoing and flamboyant. She was also ashamed that she had never been able to live up to her mother's expectations of her being a Southern belle [...] A woman was supposed to 'be popular' with men [...] Her divorce was just a further indication of failure.''

Marianna left New York after Hazel died to find a job that offered some real security. She worked for many years for the Bureau of Indian Affairs, overseeing their early childhood education programs. A thrifty woman who never wanted to be a burden on her family, she financed her own retirement to an assisted living facility well before it was necessary and was beloved by everyone there.[157]

Probably because of her aunt's strong sense of privacy, Mia was never told anything about her aunt's friend, Hazel. At the time that Marianna knew Hazel, Mia was growing up, going to high school in Connecticut.

Whatever Marianna and Hazel had meant to one another, Mia had no idea.

It is very clear that Hazel bequeathed generously to those she loved. For a woman who seemed to be so consumed with going after the money that she felt belonged to her, she nonetheless seemed quite expansive with her wealth as she made out her last will and testament. In addition to the women listed above, Hazel also gave money to Ivory Wyatt, who I believe served as a maid in Hazel's household growing up, and Flora Palumbo Dane, a gifted former opera singer who I suspect may have been Hazel's voice teacher when she and my father lived in New York.

It is worth noting that Hazel's greatest generosity was shown, not to any single individual, but rather, to three charities. To the New York Institute for the Education of the Blind and to The Seeing Eye, Inc., she gave $2,000 and $8,000, respectively.[158] These institutions were bowled over by these gifts, worth considerably more than those amounts at the time of the bequests. Perhaps Hazel's interest in helping the blind was motivated by her friendship with Tom. He had served on the board of a society aiding the blind.

Hazel also left $30,000 to the Memorial Center for Cancer and Allied Diseases,[159] now well-known as The Sloan-Kettering Institute for Cancer Research. It seems very likely that this gift was motivated by the pain of seeing her mother succumb to this terrible illness. In today's dollars, her gift was approximately equivalent to an astonishing $300,000. Whatever else her flaws and failures, Hazel ensured that she left something lasting to an organization that has done a great deal of good, and that continues to do so.

Mr. McCabe Goes To Washington

My father moved to Washington, D.C. to live alone.

It isn't clear to me if, in July of 1945, he and Hazel were still ostensibly a couple, living apart because of Dad's job but visiting one another often, or if they had by then severed all ties. Either way, this new residence would be a place where my father would spend most of his days by himself. He had returned from his overseas work with UNRRA and began working for that same organization in the United States.[160] He had likely wanted Hazel to move to Washington with him, and she had refused. Even if they were still technically a couple at the time of the move, Dad must have had a strong sense that something was very wrong.

Instead of renting an apartment, which must have seemed to him too permanent a choice, and an admission that his marriage was over, Dad took a room at an apartment hotel located at 1509 16th Street, N.W.[161] This hotel was located very near to UNRRA's Washington office, so it also seems to have been a practical choice. It would have been an easy walk to work every morning.

I imagine his time here must have been one of the loneliest and the saddest of his life. Did Hazel ever visit him, or was his room there always a place of solitude? He moved in during the month of July 1945 and didn't move out until September of 1948. By that date, their marriage had been annulled. It would seem that at this point, he would have given up all hope of any reconciliation with Hazel.

And yet, surprisingly, his next move was not to find a more permanent residence in D.C. but rather a return to New York. It might have been a move made only out of necessity. His job with UNRRA had been terminated, not because of any failing on Dad's part, but rather because UNRRA had brought its work to a conclusion. The war was long over. The need it had filled was no longer as pressing as it had been back in the mid-1940s.

He spent what must have been a very long and depressing nine months unemployed. Or, as he phrased it on his resume, "self-employed." Maybe he was actually doing some sort of work for pay at that time; it seems entirely possible, however, that he was down on his luck, living off of savings, and brokenhearted over the end of his marriage. That winter must have stretched itself out before him like a long, dark cave, one that he had to enter, even though he didn't know if there would ever be light at the end of any of its cold passages.

The annulment case was heard in December of 1947, and at Hazel's behest, the marriage was legally terminated. In August of 1948, Dad took an opportunity available to him because of his association with UNRRA. A position opened up as a statistician at the United Nations headquarters in Lake Success, NY. He moved to Queens Village, no more than half an hour from where Hazel was living in Manhattan.[162]

I can't help but wonder if he had hoped they might reconcile. One of my father's short stories that I have found among his things is entitled "A New Look For Lydia." In it the characters of Lydia and Barney Eldridge are separated, their marriage in ruins. Barney returns to Lydia's life, and by the end, she has reconsidered their breakup, and it is clear that they will reunite.[163] But in Dad's real story, there was no reconciliation. The job at the U.N. did not work out. Whether the decision to quit that job was Dad's or the U.N.'s, I have no idea. I know only that he said that the position turned out to be something other than what he had been led to expect. And so began another period of "self-employment," one that stretched from March of 1950 into the autumn of that year.

Finally, an opportunity opened up with his former employer, the U.S. Department of Agriculture. It would mean a return to Washington, a move that would take him far from Hazel, from any hope of seeing her or running into her on the streets of Manhattan. Perhaps he had finally reached a point where this was a welcome idea. Or perhaps he left New York reluctantly, full of anxiety that this would effectively end all hope of ever reuniting with her. I can't be sure, but I do know that the lodging choice he made when he returned to D.C., the Cairo Hotel, was not the choice of someone who was ready to settle down and put down roots in a new city.

Completed in 1894, the Cairo became D.C.'s tallest residential building and was eye-catching for more than just its height; its face boasts gargoyles, winged griffins, elephant heads, and dragons. The hotel became a centerpiece of D.C. nightlife, and at the time Dad lived there, the hotel would have been hopping with music, dancing, and glittering revelers into the wee hours of the morning.

I don't know why my father elected to stay at the Cairo. Perhaps he was drawn there by the long list of luminaries who had been guests over the years, one of whom was Thomas Edison. As my father sat in his Cairo room, typing the play that would become *Waverly Place* or one of the other scripts or stories he worked away at each night after work, it must have appealed to him to know that F. Scott Fitzgerald had done the same thing during his stays at the Cairo.

I can't help but try to imagine my father at this city landmark, at the time famed for the Sunday mambo parties. I like to imagine that he availed himself of a social life awaiting him just a few floors down, meeting and dancing with women, attempting to put Hazel behind him. But then I also imagine him spending evenings alone, lost in his own remembering.

It's hard for me to say who my father might have been while he stayed at the Cairo. The man I knew when I was a child was fun-loving, gregarious, the life of any gathering, an incurable joke-teller. If my father was ever morose, bitter, tormented, during the years I was growing up, he hid it completely from me and my sister. But I never knew the man who lived alone in Washington during that long winter of 1950-51. I can make no educated guess about the way he behaved. I had never witnessed my father brokenhearted and beaten. Whether he succumbed to it or camouflaged his sadness is a mystery I cannot solve.

*   *   *

My father was living at the Cairo in February of 1951. It had been a strange, unsettled period of weather in Washington that month. The beginning of February had seen bitterly cold temperatures unusual for D.C., but by February 27th, the day my father walked into the State Department on a mission, the temperature was nearly 70 degrees.[164] Dad had likely shed his overcoat and was perspiring in his suit jacket, which he certainly would not have removed, as he wanted to create a respectable impression on the people he was about to meet.

Somehow he had seen, or been shown, an article about Hazel's death printed in a Mexican newspaper. The State Department employee who drafted the memo of his appearance at their office wrote that he "seemed quite upset over the death of his former wife."[165] Was his agitation attributable merely to the shock and sorrow any of us would feel at hearing someone we had once loved had died, or was his reaction as severe as it was because he had, against all common sense, harbored hope that someday he and Hazel might reconcile?

I will never be able to be certain, but I think it a remarkably revealing fact that, the very month after Hazel's death, after a long period of living in the transient, impermanent housing of hotels, my father at last moved from the Cairo and signed a year's lease on an apartment on Randolph Street, N.W.[166]

Hazel was gone forever. And it was time for him to move on.

*   *   *

My parents met in the early spring of 1954. Hazel had been dead for three years. I don't know for certain, of course, but I don't believe my father would have been spending all of those years alone. After the grief he surely experienced over Hazel's loss, I imagine he began to heal and to date. My father was a very social man, and I can't picture him holed up and alone indefinitely, even though he had been hurt by all that had happened. But even after three years, he had not yet found a woman he wanted to get serious with.

My mother was twelve years younger than my father. She had been married at twenty-one to a young pilot she met at an Air Force base in Alabama during World War II, but their marriage had lasted less than a year. Lieutenant Robert Miller was shot down and killed over France, leaving my mother a very young and heartbroken widow. For a time, Mom moved out to Hollywood, California to live with her husband's sister but eventually moved back to Alabama to live with her mother.

Mom had told me about this early marriage the very same day that she told me about Dad and Hazel. Discovering that both of my parents had lived lives that I had been completely unaware of was a startling revelation for me. I could tell by the little she told me about her marriage to Bob that she had been deeply in love with him. She seemed to try to minimize that, however, when she told the story, perhaps worrying that I might think she had not been as in love with Dad as she had been with this first husband.

I added up the years between Bob's death and her marriage to Dad. "So, you spent twelve years of your life without anyone?"

Mom looked down and smiled, remembering something or someone she did not tell me about that day. "Well, I waited twelve years to get married again."

My parents both worked at the Department of Agriculture. Mom and my grandmother had moved to Washington in the early 1950s so that Mom could get a federal job, and they could be near my mother's brother, my Uncle Curtis. According to the story my mother told me, Dad first spied her outside the USDA one afternoon and asked a friend if he knew who "that pretty woman" was.

"That's Hazel Miller," the friend said.

Dad later told Mom how his heart had sunk at that news. Hazel! How uncanny and off-putting it was for her to have the same name as the woman who had hurt him so badly. He wanted to make a fresh start and not be reminded of the past.

Nevertheless, he pushed that aside and asked her out. Their romance took off quickly, and they married a little over a year later, in May of 1955.

After all that I have learned about that first Hazel, I can see that the two women were about as unalike as they could possibly be. Hazel Kramer was quite tall, and my mother was of average height. According to all accounts, the first Hazel was vivacious, talkative, loud, and a real "personality," whereas Mom was soft-spoken, shy, and what my father referred to as "ladylike." Mom was a lifelong Methodist, attending church every Sunday, and participating in church functions. Unlike his first Hazel, Mom was an accomplished cook, seamstress, and homemaker. She didn't smoke; she rarely drank. She was careful with money, having grown up quite poor. Could these dramatic differences have been one of the reasons that my father asked her to marry him?

My mother was no saint. She had a sly and sarcastic wit that snuck up on you when you least expected it, and she was a fierce protector of those she loved. She didn't hesitate to fight for things or people if she thought something was wrong or unfair. But nonetheless, it seems to me that she was a very different person than Hazel Kramer.

Dad had walked a long way down what he must have thought was the wrong road. With my mother, he headed off in an entirely new direction. Together, they created the family that my father had always wanted. Both had feared they would never have children, but fate gave them both a second chance at happiness. It came to them late, but it came.

Letting Go

The night before my father went into the hospital, he looked up from his reading, which I'm sure he was only half-looking at anyway, and asked me a question that so startled me, I have never forgotten it.

"Mel," he said, "are you afraid to die?"

Even at the age of sixteen, a young girl, I knew this was not the sort of question a father was supposed to ask his daughter. It alerted me instantly to some things about my father that I had not previously known, or at least, had not understood: that he was mortal, that he feared this operation he was about to have, that he felt close enough to me to ask such a question and, perhaps, did not feel able to ask such a question of my mother.

And somehow, I knew, too, that the appropriate response would be to say something reassuring, to help my father to feel less afraid. But in those few words he had spoken to me something that was true and unguarded. I could not give him back anything less.

"Yes," I said. "I am." I paused, waited. Then added, "Are you?"

He nodded. "Yes."

We looked at each other, without words, and I put my hand over his.

And then something changed. It was as though the Angel of Parental Discretion and Reason had laid a hand on his shoulder to remind him that he had ventured into a realm where it was inappropriate to take one's child. The mood shifted. He made light of his anxieties, seeing the concern in my eyes.

"Just listen to your old man, being melodramatic!" he said. "Now don't tell my doctor what a big crybaby I'm being—or that I impugned his medical skills. And for God's sakes, don't tell your mother."

It was the last time I ever spoke to him.

In all the years since that day, I have often wondered what sort of relationship my father and I might have formed had we had the chance. I never got the opportunity to know him fully. He made certain that my sister and I did not glimpse any of his failures or weaknesses. He steered us swiftly away from his "dark places."

What's more, my father knew me only as a young girl. I was just beginning to leave childhood behind when he died. What signs of impending womanhood and independent selfhood I had shown seemed to threaten him more than please him. As a little girl, I would always be entirely his, worshipful of the father who to me was bigger than life. But my growing up was already beginning to jeopardize that. I was pulling away from him, as teenagers are supposed to do. I think that, somehow, to my father, this felt almost like a betrayal. It was plain to see at times that my disengagement hurt him.

After he died, the guilt I felt about that stayed with me a very long time. Perhaps to a certain extent, I feel it still.

*   *   *

It was a gray and bitterly cold day in January of 1974. My father had been dead a little over a month and the chasm that his loss had opened in my life was enormous. My childhood up until that moment had been charmed. I lived in an insulated world with two parents who adored me, and what worries or sorrows I had known were petty, temporary, and easily forgotten. I had believed utterly in the magical story of my life, had felt invulnerable to whatever tragedies befell people outside of the bubble of my daily routine.

That my father had died, had not been saved by any of my bargaining with God, or by the contract I thought had been signed with the universe when I was born, shook me to my very core. No one was safe. I was not safe. And no one could understand the profound sadness and deep regret that fell like a veil over everything I had once believed about the world.

That afternoon I slipped noiselessly down into my father's basement office. Its walls, its desk, its papers, untouched by anyone since he had disappeared into the white fluorescence, the antiseptic air that had swallowed him whole and refused to give him back again. The sealed space full of my father's things brimmed with his scent, with the evidence that he had lived and hoped and typed and filed and jotted and loved.

Atop the shelf at one end of the room were his two Abraham Lincoln bookends – metal casts of Abe as he appears at the Lincoln Memorial. When I was a little girl, these bookends were part of the elaborate ritual my father had concocted for seeing me to bed each night. At a certain point in that nightly process, Dad would ask me, "Shall we go say goodnight to Mr. Lincoln?" And we would descend the stairs; I, held in his arms, so that I might gravely wish the former president "sweet dreams," and pat the top of his shiny bronze hair.

On another wall was a caricature someone had once drawn of Dad: a profile view, his mouth drawn into an exaggerated grin, his nose prominent, his eyes squeezed shut into crescent moons, and his one visible ear enormous, absurdly outsized, I suppose to indicate his profound hearing loss. Beneath the image were the words, "McCabe, Chi Phi, Campus Pianist." I had looked at that drawing nearly every day of my childhood, never knowing that one day in 2013, I would find its mate: a caricature drawn of Hazel by the same artist. What a surprise it had been to come upon her image and to realize that once these two drawings had hung side by side. I wonder now if my father remembered this other drawing every time his eyes fell on the one of himself.

That January day, I seemed to have a mission, though I doubt I could have articulated it had anyone asked. I closed Dad's office door, sat down in his large chair, and as quietly as I could, pulled open the top drawer of his Army-green metal filing cabinet and began to go through the evidence of my father's life, file by file. I was not looking for any one specific thing; I was looking for pieces of who my father was, pieces that, if I put them together, would bring him back to me, would show me the man that had been stolen from me before I could fully know him.

Today I remember only two findings from that long-ago quest. I found a letter that my father had written to Elia Kazan, about one of Dad's plays that he had apparently sent to this famous director. At the time, I had no idea who Elia Kazan was, but I remembered the name because it was so unusual. And I found another letter Dad had written to the Mayo Clinic about treatment for his hearing loss, outlining all that he had previously tried and asking if there was anything that could be done to help him.

I have strained my memory to bring back any other fact that came out of that stealthy search. I remember the black ink that rubbed off on my fingertips from the carbons, the musty scent of the tissue-thin pages, the envelopes that had half-resealed themselves in the damp air of our basement. I had taken great pains to reopen them without leaving any telltale rips. But I cannot summon to my memory any more of the secrets that might have been revealed to me that day.

I did not know on that afternoon that there had ever been another Hazel. If I had seen letters or documents referencing someone named Hazel McCabe, or letters to Dad from someone named Hazel, I would of course have assumed they were about or from my mother. When I think of all that I might have read that day, all of the answers I might have held in my hands, unaware of what they meant, I can barely stand it. So great is this ache and urge to understand my father's past, I even briefly considered hypnosis.

"Do you suppose if I was hypnotized, by someone reputable, I might remember things I read about that day?" I asked Chris.

He looked dubious. And after I considered it a bit, I conceded that I felt pretty dubious about it myself. And so I did no more than think about it. But that day has haunted me, as has the terrible truth that my mother took all of those files and threw them away. Was there anything that I could do to resurrect those years? When was it time to surrender, to admit that I might well have found out everything about Dad and Hazel that there was to know?

* * *

Who have I become in these last four years?

A 2017 version of a film noir gumshoe, skulking the dark, rain-wet streets in my fedora and trench coat. I am always searching, for some sign, some name, some document that will reveal to me a piece of the mystery. I spend my time in the shadows and the wee hours, up too late prowling the internet for something new, something I may have missed the last time I looked.

Hours of late-night internet sleuthing will sometimes yield names of people that I can find in the present day. And when I receive a reply, it always feels to me both startling and thrill-ing— just the way I imagine an archaeologist must feel when unearthing some previously unknown species.

But it takes all of my diplomatic skills and finesse to compose queries that do not alarm but instead, reassure, intrigue, and ultimately, seduce.

In the present day, in my "real" life, I am not a gregarious individual. I am not unfriendly, by any means, but I would never be called outgoing. In any large gathering, I am most often on the sidelines. At a party, I linger against the wall. And so casting myself as the instigator of conversations, the aggressor, goes quite against type.

It is a new role that I still have not quite grown used to.

And when I find clues, connections to the past, I am quite aware that when I reach out to them, send off an inquiry, that my message must rise up in their inbox or from their stack of mail like some eerie missive from the grave. I have put myself in their shoes, have imagined how I would feel, react, if I were to receive a message from a stranger about some long-dead member of my family. How unsettling would it be to receive a letter from an unknown person who seemed to have an uncanny wealth of details about the events and relationships of my family's past?

I can see how it might alarm me. Was I being scammed? Stalked? Was this some gambit for personal information that would be used to take advantage of me in some way? But I think that on some level, I would be both excited and intrigued. I love history, exploring the past, unearthing secrets. Such a query would most certainly appeal to me on that level.

At times, I will send out messages, and nothing returns to me. In these cases, I never know if I reached the wrong person, or someone deceased, or whether the recipient simply found my letter suspect and not something to which he or she wished to reply. These queries into the Vast Void are par for the course.

What is incredible to me is how many times I have met with success. Against all odds, I have received quite a lot of replies from people who seem genuinely excited to hear from me. Often, the respondent tells me that she had always wanted to explore her families' pasts but hadn't found the time. Or that he hadn't thought of Great Aunt So-and-So in years, and that his memories had been revived by my letter.

These successful efforts are what keep me going. Not only in my own research, but in my assurance that the work that I have done serves to resurrect, not just my father and Hazel, but many people long dead.

And there has been something else that has pushed me to pursue every aspect of this that I can: I had promised this book not only to myself, but also to my sister, Terri.

That promise took on new urgency in the autumn of 2014 when we learned that Terri's cancer had metastasized, and that it was very unlikely that she had much longer to live. No one had cared more about this project than she had. Each new discovery I made was thrilling to her as we tried to take the new pieces of the puzzle and fit them together to create the father we had never known.

Just two months before we got the terrible news of her prognosis, Terri had sat with me in my living room and read through the first six chapters of this book. She asked questions, she cried out in surprise, she laughed, she shook her head in amazement. In short, she *reacted* to this story that mattered so much to both of us. When she finished, she said, "This is great, Mel. I can't wait to read the whole book."

Although now she never will, I am determined that the story must exist. If there is any afterlife, then perhaps, somehow, she will know. And if there is not, well, at least I will know that I did what I told her I would do.

Long ago, it was Terri that convinced my mother to crack open the lock to the trunk that held all of my father's secrets, all of the memorabilia from his marriage to Hazel. Terri was avidly curious and relentless in all that she did in this life, and I find that, in this way, I am very like my sister. This story was just a bigger lock that needed breaking. And so, I have given it my best shot.

*   *   *

Tennessee Williams lived a great deal of his life on paper. He wrote frequent letters, he kept a journal, he transformed the events of his existence into plays, stories, and poems. And so I searched hard for some written evidence of Tom's discovery that his beloved friend Hazel had died.

I have found nothing in his letters or journal entries. This seems to me nothing short of incredible. Given how strong his feelings were for her, right up until the last years of his life, surely he would have reached out to a friend or family member to share his shock, his sorrow, and his loss. Where was Tom when he heard the news? Did he read it himself in a Mexican newspaper? Did a friend see an article and pass it along to him? Did someone telephone him to break it to him as gently as possible?

I have wondered whether it might have been my father who sent him word. Dad learned of her death a little over a week after it happened. Did he think about Tom, Hazel's dear childhood friend?

Certainly, I believe my father saw Williams as a kind of a role model, and that he would have admired him enough to want to send him word. Dad noted Tom's great success, and knowing what I do of my father, I can imagine how he must have coveted it. In researching my father's past, I found a notice in *The Washington Post* advertising a "Playwright Course" being offered by the Department of Agriculture Graduate School.[167] The course was taught by my father. Surely, he must have seen himself as a playwright; he must have believed himself knowledgeable enough to impart wisdom to others. The course was offered in the winter of 1952. Hazel had been gone for only a year.

When Dad died in 1973, Tennessee Williams knew about it. He mentions Dad's death in *Something Cloudy, Something Clear*. And he certainly must have known that Dad had died before he named a character Terrence McCabe in *The Red Devil Battery Sign*. But if any record exists of my father writing to Williams, or of someone writing to Williams about my father, I have not been lucky enough to find it. I have had to let go of my quest for it.

There have been many hopes, many treasure hunts, which have propelled me forward in these last two years. Always it seemed to me that just a day or two ahead of me was the shimmering possibility of finding the letter or the person who could reveal everything that had been hidden in the shadows of the past. The quest for these "holy grails" has consumed many an evening when I needed to be attending to other things, many a weekend when I might have been outside on a glorious sunny afternoon, reveling in the world and in the people I love.

Near the beginning of this project, I communicated with an author who had written a book very similar to the one I hoped to write about Hazel and my father. I praised the book she had produced, and she told me that the research for it had taken her ten years. Ten years! I thought about what it would mean to devote the next ten years of my life to uncovering the facts behind Hazel's sad story, behind the hurts that had influenced who my father became. So many other writing projects would have to be postponed or abandoned, projects that I wanted very much to begin. As much as I wanted to solve the riddles I had discovered, I did not want to give a decade of my life to the effort.

And so, there have been things that I have had to let go. I have given up my pursuit of Tom's letters to Hazel's lawyer, William Crowdus. I looked in all of the major Williams' archives, I searched through every page of the *McCabe v. Bagby* court documents, I even tracked down William Crowdus's grandson in the hopes that some old trunk or file remained that would contain these coveted documents. But I found nothing. Did William Crowdus or his secretary throw these letters away once the trial was concluded? Or did Crowdus hang on to the letters as a keepsake? Tennessee Williams was by then quite famous, and Crowdus might have considered that the letters might well be worth something in the future.

I also had to wave the white flag in my pursuit of Russell Henderson Burke and any hope of certainty I might have of his relationship with Hazel. So, too, have I had to abandon the idea that I would ever gain certainty about the way she felt about women. Or even the way that she felt about my father.

Still, there are moments where someone else's observations seem to make things just a little clearer. Just the other day, I again picked up Edwina Williams' memoir, *Remember Me to Tom*. I had combed through it avidly when I had first obtained it, thinking that surely Tom's mother might have plenty to say about Hazel, the girl who had stolen her son's heart. It is a hard book to search through, because there is no index. There was no other recourse but skimming through each and every page, searching for the name "Hazel."

I quickly found again the mention of Hazel that I had discovered the first time through:

> Ever since he was twelve, Tom had known and liked a girl named Hazel Kramer...By the time he reached his last year in high school, they had become very close...Hazel was imbued with a joy for living...one of the most wholesome girls I have ever met...The friendship between her and Tom might have ripened into romance if Cornelius had not interfered because he didn't think Hazel good enough for Tom.[168]

There was nothing in this that told me anything I had not previously known, other than that Edwina found Hazel to be wholesome. During that first look at the book, I had found nothing more. But the other day, I found a passage near the end that I had not seen before: "Tom told me Hazel visited him after the success of his plays and confessed her marriage was a miserable one. She has since died."[169]

In a letter that Tom's good friend Esmeralda Mayes wrote to Tom in 1963, she mentions his mother's book and says, "I truly feel that she was somewhat unfair to Hazel. Poor, dear, beautiful and spoiled Hazel."[170]

I wondered what Esmeralda meant by that. Certainly calling Hazel wholesome could not be construed as unfair, so I assumed that what she was referring to was his remark about Hazel telling Tom that her marriage was "a miserable one." Edwina's statement backs up what Tom wrote in the original typescript of *Something Cloudy, Something Clear*, in which the Hazel character tells August that only the first six months of her marriage to Terrence McCabe were happy ones, and that after that, she stayed only out of loyalty.[171]

Did Esmeralda think that this statement was untrue? In which case, she should put the blame on Tom, and not Edwina, who was only reporting what had been told to her. Or did she think that Edwina was unfair for bringing up something that should have remained private?

If I say that I have a hard time imagining how marriage to my father might have been a miserable experience, could I possibly seem like anything other than a protective daughter, eager to convey only a positive image of the father she adored? Probably not. But nonetheless, I do find it hard to believe. My father could be stubborn. Opinionated. He loved to joke around, sometimes to the point where he pushed it too far. He was often difficult to communicate with, because of his deafness. He had a temper and would sometimes explode in a loud and emotional verbal tantrum. But he was also a man who wore his heart on his sleeve. Deeply and unabashedly sensitive. Affectionate and playful. Smart and well-informed. Unfailingly loyal to anyone he loved. Maybe the man who was married to Hazel was not the man who raised me for the first sixteen years of my life. But then, Tennessee Williams had much the same idea of my father that I had when he called him personable, likable, and good-humored.

I don't know how my father could have caused Hazel misery. I think she was an unhappy woman, but I do not believe that this unhappiness was my father's doing, at least not directly. She was unhappy because her mother was a manipulative bully who was possessive of her daughter and did not want to lose the close bond they shared. She may well have been unhappy because my father's success was slow in coming, and for many years they lived a very hand-to-mouth existence. She may have been increasingly unhappy as her alcoholism took over her life. And she certainly may have felt real sorrow if she found herself in love with someone else—whether that someone was Russell Burke or one of her female friends with whom she had such close ties.

How can I judge a relationship, a marriage, I have no real knowledge of? I cannot. As someone who has been through her own divorces, I know quite well that what the outside world perceives to be true may not bear any resemblance to what actually happened. I know that people harbor secret selves that others may never guess at. I will not pretend to understand my father's first marriage. But I have my own theories about it.

I believe that Hazel was happy with my father for longer than she claimed. I think it may well have suited her purposes to claim otherwise on that long-ago day when she met with Tom to secure his help in her challenge of Emma's will. She wanted him to sympathize with her, to help her. Her mindset about my father in 1947 might also have colored for her all the memories of the ten years they had lived together as husband and wife.

I do not cast blame. Maybe if I had learned more than I did, I would have a reason to. But I think not. I feel a strange tenderness toward Hazel, a difficult-to-explain protectiveness of her. No one who knew her or loved her is here to speak for her anymore. So I will take on that task. She was an emotional, hopeful, romantic, exuberant, and loving woman whose troubles proved too great for her to bear. She made mistakes. She fell prey to weaknesses. She was human. Maybe my father never forgave her. But I do.

*   *   *

I am a different woman now than I was the day Chris first told me that Tennessee Williams had named one of his characters Terrence McCabe.

When I began my research, all I knew was that my father had a first wife, who was loved by Tennessee Williams, who died mysteriously in a foreign country, possibly in the company of another man. After two years, I have discovered so much more, some of it, I hope, of interest to anyone who follows the life and career of this great American playwright. I have a more complete understanding of just how important Hazel was to her friend Tom, and how that relationship extended many years past when most biographers assume that it ended. I have filled in much more of the story of Hazel Kramer's life and learned something of Williams' feelings about my father, through Williams' letters, journals, and his creation of a character modeled after Dad in *The Red Devil Battery Sign*.

On a smaller scale, I have gained information that is of great personal consequence to me. If someone had asked me on that day in May 2013 about my father, I would have said that I loved him deeply, and that not a day went by that I did not remember him.

But that would have been a lie.

The truth was that many days went by in which I did not think about my father at all. More than forty years had passed since I had lost him, and in those many years, the vividness of my memories had grown blurry, and the man that I recalled had taken on the nature of a myth, a tale told over and over again but each time, less real and more just a story.

I had had him in my life for only sixteen years, and the man I knew at times seemed like something I had invented, a character I had created through years of talking about him with my mother, my sister. He was compartmentalized, on a shelf with other old memories, and I took that memory down only occasionally. I had moved on with my life.

But in the last two years, my father has reentered my world. In my journey into his past—his letters, his photographs, his writings – I have come to know a man I only half-knew before. I have met the boy, the young man falling in love, the new husband, the scorned lover, and the broken divorcee who wondered if his life would ever be happy again. I have come so much closer to knowing who he really was. I have had my father back again.

No matter what else occurred in those years that I never knew—no matter what misunderstandings or bitter feelings or sins are a part of that history—this quest has made all of that seem insignificant in comparison.

I have a rounder, fuller picture of the father I lost so early in my life. In the years that I have worked on this project, my father has, in a very real sense, returned to me. In reading through his creative work and his letters, in going back over all of his old photos, I have felt my father's presence beside me, urging me on. I lost him when I was just sixteen years old: not yet a woman who could meet him and love him on equal ground. Researching and writing this book has changed that. I have looked at my father, eye-to-eye, and he has looked back at me.

This is the legacy that Hazel Kramer and Tennessee Williams have left to me. I owe them a great debt.

SELECTED BIBLIOGRAPHY

UNPUBLISHED SOURCES

Alter, Stewart. McCann-Erickson. Email to Melanie McCabe. September 16, 2015.

Ancestry.com, various sources.

Bak, John. E-mails to Melanie McCabe, May 20 and June 26, 2013.

Bagby, Cindy. Email to Melanie McCabe. June 9, 2014.

Bagby, Debbie. Facebook message to Melanie McCabe, September 22, 2014.

Bagby, Nancy. Phone conversation. June, 2014.

Barclay, Francine. Phone conversation. July 24, 2015.

Bray, Robert. Email to Melanie McCabe, June 28, 2013.

Burke, Russell Henderson. Death Certificate. State of California.

Campagna, Lory White. Emails to Melanie McCabe. August 16 and September 18, 2013.

Crowdus, William to Tennessee Williams, correspondence, June 3, 1947.

Ferris, Harold A. Email to Melanie McCabe, August 11, 2015.

Frost, Michael. Manuscripts & Archives, Yale University. Email. February 11, 2014.

Fulghum, Leigh. Email to Melanie McCabe. August 19, 2015.

Gibson, Esme. Email to Melanie McCabe. July 6, 2013.

Glus, Barbara Bern. Email to Melanie McCabe. September 30, 2013.

Graham, Marycarroll Dane. Phone conversation. July 2014.

Henderson, Bruce. Email to Melanie McCabe. August 4 and 11, 2015.

Horrell, Martin to Terrence McCabe. Correspondence. October 11, 1945.

Hughes, Thomas R. Correspondence to Melanie McCabe. June 22, 2014.

Keane, Eleanor. Phone conversation. May 9, 2015.

Kramer, Emma, in the Matter of the Estate Of. State of Michigan in the Probate Court for the County of Oakland, March 4, 1948.

Langbart, David. National Archives. Email. July 19, 2013.

Link, Michael. Email to Melanie McCabe. July 31, 2013.

Marlatt, Ginger. Email to Melanie McCabe. August 31, 2013.

Marlatt, Ginger. Phone conversation. September, 2013.

Mather, Mia. Email to Melanie McCabe. July 22, 2015.

McCabe, Hazel Elizabeth White. Death Certificate, National Archives.

McCabe, Hazel to Tennessee Williams, correspondence, May 18, 1947.

McCabe, Hazel E. Last Will & Testament, September 1, 1950.

McCabe, Hazel E. In Matter of Estate of Hazel E. McCabe. March 16, 1951.

McCabe, Hazel Elizabeth White. Reports of Deaths of American Citizens Abroad, National Archives.

McCabe, Terrence W. Brief autobiography. An unpublished manuscript.

McCabe, Terrence W. The Distant Hill. An unpublished manuscript.

McCabe, Terrence W. "A New Look For Lydia," unpublished short story.

McCabe, Terrence W. A Superior View. An unpublished manuscript.

McCabe, Terrence W. U.S. Department of Agriculture Employment File.

McCabe, Terrence W. Waverly Place. Unpublished play. New York Public Library Theatre Collection.

McCabe v. Bagby, transcript of court case, District Court of the United States for the Eastern District of Michigan, Southern Distict, 1948.

McCabe v. Bagby, transcript, Appeal, District Court of the United States for the Eastern District of Michigan, Southern Distict, 1950.

Miller, Peter. Email to Melanie McCabe. August 18, 2014.

Molina, Fernando. Email to Melanie McCabe. July 29, 2013.

Morningstar, Roberta McCabe. Phone conversation. July 2013.

Oak Grove Mausoleum, St. Louis, MO, phone call, July, 2013.

O'Connor, Donald J. Email to Melanie McCabe. July 17, 2013.

Perkowski, Chris. Email to Melanie McCabe. February 28, 2013.

Queens County Courthouse. Phone conversation. January, 2014.

Treen, Esmeralda Mayes to Tennessee Williams, Correspondence. May 9, 1963. New Orleans Collection.

Vaughan, Jackie. Email to Melanie McCabe. October, 2015.

Wilkie, Joan Romadka. Correspondence to Melanie McCabe. August 17, 2015.

Williams, Francesca. Email to Melanie McCabe. October 26, 2015.

Williams, Tennessee. Something Cloudy, Something Clear. Unpublished typescript. Ohio State University library.

PUBLISHED SOURCES

Atlanta Constitution. Five articles. January 17, 1937; June 27, 1937; August 30, 1938; February 6, 1939. February 9, 1939.

Bak, John S. Tennessee Williams: A Literary Life. New York: Palgrave MacMillan, 2013.

Devlin, Albert J. (ed). Conversations With Tennessee Williams. Jackson, MS: University Press of Mississippi, 1986.

Dance Magazine. Photo. November, 1949.

Excelsior. Mexico City, Mexico. "Extraña Muerte de Norte-americana, White McCabe", February 17, 1951.

Hale, Allean. "Tennessee Williams' St. Louis Blues"

Leverich, Lyle. Tom: The Unknown Tennessee Williams. New York: W.W. Norton & Co., 1995.

El Nacional, Mexico City. Mexico. "Misteriosa Muerte de Agraciada Dama," February 17, 1951.

New York Times. "Fire At A Brooklyn Warehouse Puts Private Lives on Display", February 1, 2015.

New York Times, Advertising News & Notes, December 20, 1947; February 10, 1950; December, 1950.

Prosser, William. The Late Plays of Tennessee Williams. Scarecrow Press, 2008

St. Louis Post Dispatch, "Law Clerk's Wife Who Sues Husband On Cruelty Charge," January 22, 1913.

St. Louis Post Dispatch, "Wife In Divorce Suit Says Lawyer Upset Furniture," June 9, 1913.

St. Louis Post Dispatch, "Divorces Husband Whom She Found As Cold As Ice," June 10, 1913.

Thomas, Romayne Lutter. Obituary. Ozaukee Press, Port Washington, WI. October, 2007.

Thornton, Margaret Bradham (ed). Notebooks; Tennessee Williams. New Haven, CT: Yale University Press, 2006.

Universal Grafico. Mexico City, Mexico. "Extraña Muerte..." February 16, 1951.

Williams, Dakin. His Brother's Keeper. Collinsville, IL: Dakin's Corner Press, 1983.

Williams, Edwina. Remember Me To Tom. New York: G.P. Putnam's Sons, 1963.

Williams, Tennessee. Memoirs. New York: Doubleday & Co., Inc., 1975.

Williams, Tennessee. The Red Devil Battery Sign. New York. New Directions Books. 1975.

Williams, Tennessee. The Theatre of Tennessee Williams, Volume III. New York: New Directions Books, 1992.

Windham, Donald. *Lost Friendships: A Memoir of Truman Capote, Tennessee Williams and Others*. United Kingdom. Athena Press, 1989.

ENDNOTES

1. Ibid., p. 38.

2. Ibid., p. 230.

3. www.lifetimetv.co.uk biographybiography-pierce-brosnan

4. McCabe, from short, unpublished autobiography

5. McCabe, *A Superior View*, unpublished manuscript.

6. Devlin, *Conversations With Tennessee Williams*, p. 230

7. Williams, *Memoirs*, p. 15.

8. Leverich, *Tom*, p. 146.

9. Williams, Dakin. *His Brother's Keeper*, pp. 28-29.

10. Leverich, op.cit., p. 72.

11. Bak, *Tennessee Williams: A Literary Life*, p. 17.

12. John S. Bak, email, May 20, 2013.

13. John S. Bak, email, June 26, 2013.

14. Robert Bray, email, June 28, 2013.

15. Ibid.

16. Thornton, *Notebooks*, p. 105.

17. Ibid., p. 104.

18. Ibid., p. 753.

19. Ibid, pp. xxx

20. Ibid., p. 4.

21. Ibid., p. 8.

22. Ibid., p. x

23. Williams, *Memoirs*, p. 29.

24. Windham, Donald. *Lost Friendships: A Memoir of Truman Capote, Tennessee Williams and Others*. United Kingdom. Athena Press, 1989.

25. Williams, *The Red Devil Battery Sign*, pp. 31-32.

26. Ibid., pp. 58-59.

27. Ibid., p. 38.

28. Ibid., p. 66.

29. Ibid., pp.66-67.

30. Ibid., p. 76.

31. Leverich, op.cit., p. 54

32. McCabe v. Bagby, transcript of court case, 1948. National Archives, Chicago Branch.

33. St. Louis Post Dispatch, June 10, 1913.

34. St. Louis Post Dispatch, January 22, 1913.

35. Florence Kramer White v. Franklin Madison White, Divorce proceedings transcript, May 9, 1913.

36. St. Louis Post Dispatch, June 9, 1913.

37. St. Louis Post Dispatch, June 10, 1913.

38. Ibid.

39. McCabe, *The Distant Hill*, unpublished manuscript.

40. Leverich, op.cit., p. 72.

41. McCabe, *The Distant Hill.*

42. Leverich, op.cit., p. 72.

43. Williams, Edwina. *Remember Me to Tom*, p. 60.

44. McCabe v. Bagby, court transcript, 1948. National Archives, Chicago Branch.

45. Ibid.

46. Williams, *Memoirs*, p. 15.

47. Leverich, op.cit., p. 73.

48. Leverich, op.cit., p. 72.

49. Hale, Allean. "Tennessee Williams' St. Louis Blues," *Mississippi Quarterly* 48, 4, Fall, 1995.

50. McCabe, *A Superior View.*

51. Ibid.

52. Ibid.

53. Ibid.

54. Williams, *Memoirs,* pp. 14-15.

55. McCabe, *The Distant Hill.*

56. Ibid.

57. Williams, Edwina. Op.cit., p. 42.

58. Ibid., p. xx

59. Ibid., p. 50.

60. McCabe, *A Superior View.*

61. Williams, *Memoirs,* p. 15.

62. Ibid., p. 18.

63. Ibid., p. 18.

64. McCabe, *A Superior View.*

65. Ibid.

66. Williams, Edwina. *Remember Me to Tom,* p. 60.

67. Leverich, op.cit., p. 99.

68. McCabe, *The Distant Hill.*

69. Leverich, op.cit., p. 248.

70. Francesca Williams, email, October 26, 2015.

71. McCabe, *The Distant Hill.*

72. Ibid. (Unless otherwise noted, all quoted and paraphrased material in this chapter comes from my father's unpublished manuscript, *The Distant Hill.*)

73. Correspondence, Hazel McCabe to Tennessee Williams, May 18, 1947. (Harry Ransom Center)

74. Ibid.

75. http://law.justia.com/cases/federal/appellate -courts/ F2/186/546/163198/

76. Michael Link, email, July 31, 2013.

77. Correspondence, William Crowdus to Tennessee Williams, June 3, 1947.

78. Roberta McCabe Morningstar, phone conversation, July 2013.

79. Ginger Marlatt, phone conversation, September, 2013.

80. Leverich, op.cit., pp. 535-536.

81. http://www.sos.mo.gov/images/archives/death-certs/1942/1942_00008821.PDF

82. Windham, *Lost Friendships: A Memoir of Truman Capote, Tennessee Williams and Others.*

83. Phone call, Oak Grove Mausoleum, St. Louis, MO., July, 2013.

84. Esme Gibson, email, July 6, 2013.

85. Hazel Elizabeth White McCabe, death certificate (National Archives)

86. Donald J. O'Connor, email, July 17, 2013.

87. David Langbart, National Archives, July 19, 2013.

88. Hazel Elizabeth White McCabe, Reports of Deaths of American Citizens Abroad, National Archives.

89. Ibid.

90. Ibid.

91. Ibid.

92. Ibid.

93. Ibid.

94. Ibid.

95. Ibid.

96. Fernando Molina, email, July 29, 2013.

97. *El Nacional*, "Misteriosa Muerte de Agraciada Dama," February 17, 1951.

98. *Excelsior*, "Extraña Muerte de Norteamericana, White McCabe," February 17, 1951.

99. *Universal Grafico,* "Extraña Muerte…" February 16, 1951.

100. Lory White Campagna, email, August 16, 2013.

101. Lory White Campagna, email, August 26, 2013.

102. In the Matter of the Estate of Emma Kramer, State of Michigan in the Probate Court for the County of Oakland, March 4, 1948.

103. Ibid.

104. Debbie Bagby, Facebook message, September 22, 2013.

105. Cindy Bagby, email, June 9, 2014.

106. Ibid.

107. Nancy Bagby, phone conversation, June, 2014.

108. McCabe v. Bagby, 1948. National Archives, Chicago Branch.

109. Ibid.

110. Ibid.

111. Ibid.

112. Ibid.

113. McCabe v. Bagby, appeal, 1950. National Archives, Chicago Branch.

114. Hazel E. McCabe, Last Will & Testament, September 1, 1950

115. Ancestry.com, various records

116. Michael Frost, email, Manuscripts & Archives, Yale University Alumni Association, February 11, 2014.

117. Correspondence, Martin Horrell to Terrence McCabe, October 11, 1945.

118. Ibid.

119. *New York Times*, dates.

120. Correspondence, Thomas R. Hughes, June 22, 2014.

121. Michael Frost, email, Manuscripts & Archives, Yale University Alumni Association, February 11, 2014.

122. Stewart Alter, McCann-Erickson, email, September 16, 2015.

123. Hazel E. McCabe, Tax File, Last Will & Testament, March 1951.

124. *Detroit Free Press*, Engagements, June 29, 1951.

125. *Detroit Free Press,* "Free Press Writer Kay Martin Dies," September 11, 1973.

126. Russell Henderson Burke, Death Certificate.

127. Ibid.

128. Ancestry.com, various documents

129. In The Matter of the Estate of Hazel E. McCabe, Surrogate Court, New York County, March 16, 1951.

130. Queens County Courthouse, phone call, January, 2014.

131. Chris Perkowski, email, February 28, 2014.

132. Correspondence, Emma Kramer to Hazel Bagby, from McCabe v. Bagby files, National Archives, Chicago.

133. *New York Times*, "Fire at a Brooklyn Warehouse Puts Private Lives on Display," February 1, 2015.

134. McCabe, *Waverly Place*, unpublished play. New York public Library Theatre Collection. (Unless otherwise noted, all quotations and references in this chapter come from this play script.)

135. Devlin, *Conversations With Tennessee Williams*, p. 230.

136. Prosser, William. *The Late Plays of Tennessee Williams*, p. 247.

137. Williams, unpublished typescript of *Something Cloudy, Something Clear*, Ohio State University library.

138. Ibid.

139. Ibid.

140. Williams, *Memoirs,* pp. 133-134.

141. Conversation with Eleanor Keane, May 9, 2015.

142. Ibid.

143. Conversation with Eleanor Keane, May 9, 2015.

144. Ancestry.com, various files.

145. Ibid.

146. Elizabeth Dosser obituary, *The State*, "Retired Market Researcher Miss Elizabeth Dosser Dies," February 2, 1975.

147. Obituary, Romayne Lutter Thomas, Ozaukee Press, Port Washington, Wisconsin, October, 2007.

148. Conversation with Francine Barclay, July 24, 2015.

149. 1940 U.S. Census, Ancestry.com

150. Correspondence, from Joan Romadka Wilkie, August 17, 2015.

151. Conversation with Francine Barclay

152. Ibid.

153. *Atlanta Constitution*, August 30, 1938; February 6 and 9, 1939

154. *Atlanta Constitution,* January 17, 1937; June 27, 1937.

155. *Dance Magazine*, November 1949.

156. Harold A. Ferris, email, August 11, 2015.

157. Mia Mather, email, July 22, 2015.

158. Hazel E. McCabe, Last Will & Testament, September 1, 1950.

159. Ibid.

160. Ibid.

161. Terrence W. McCabe, U.S.D.A. Employment File

162. Ibid.

163. McCabe, "A New Look for Lydia," unpublished short story.

164. *Washington Post,* February 28, 1951, weather summary.

165. Hazel Elizabeth White McCabe, Reports of Deaths of American Citizens Abroad, National Archives.

166. Terrence W. McCabe, U.S.D.A. employment file.

167. *The Washington Post*, "Playwright Course," January 27, 1952.

168. Williams, Edwina. *Remember Me to Tom.* p. 60.

169. Ibid., p. 240.

170. Correspondence, Esmeralda Mayes Treen to Tennessee Williams, May 9, 1963. (New Orleans Collection)

171. Williams, *Something Cloudy, Something Clear* original typescript, Ohio State University library.